LOOKING AT THE
Land of Promise

Pioneer Images of the Pacific Northwest

Sherman and Mabel Smith Pettyjohn Lectures in
Pacific Northwest History

LOOKING AT THE
Land of Promise

PIONEER IMAGES OF THE PACIFIC NORTHWEST

WILLIAM H. GOETZMANN

Washington State University Press
Pullman, Washington 99164-5910
1988

Washington State University Press, Pullman, Washington 99164-5910

91 90 89 88   5 4 3 2 1

Library of Congress Cataloging-in-Publication Data

Goetzmann, William H.
    Looking at the land of promise.

    Bibliography: p.
1. Northwest, Pacific, in art. 2. Art, Modern—19th century.
3. Landscape in art. I. Title.
N82l4.5.U6G62 1987   760'.04499795   87-37174
ISBN 0-87422-025-4
ISBN 0-87422-024-6 (paperback)

This book is printed on pH neutral, acid-free paper.

Cover illustration:
Mt. St. Helens from the Columbia River, 1879 by Cleveland Rockwell
Oregon Historical Society, Portland, Oregon

For Sarah Shelby and Lawrence Walker

CONTENTS

LIST OF ILLUSTRATIONS

LOOKING AT THE LAND OF PROMISE

Map of the Upper Columbia, circa 1841 by Pierre De Smet
Washington State University Libraries, Pullman, Washington

Among the earliest missionaries in the area, Father De Smet and his colleague, Nicholas Point, preached Christianity throughout the Columbia Basin and did much to publicize the Pacific Northwest to the world outside. Although De Smet is primarily known as a writer and a missionary, he was among the first Europeans to explore the Columbia Basin in a systematic fashion.

This holograph map by Father De Smet of the Columbia River and its tributaries shows locations for both Catholic and Protestant mission sites, as well as a sophisticated understanding of the drainage pattern for the Columbia Basin.

Autumn of 1841:

. . . Six miles further south we crossed the beautiful river of St. Ignatius (Hell Gate). It enters the plain of the Bitter Root—which we shall henceforward call St. Mary's—by a beautiful defile, commonly called, by the mountaineers or Canadian hunters, the Hell Gate; for what reason, however, I know not. These gentlemen have frequently on their lips the words devil and hell; and it is perhaps on this account that we heard so often these appellations. Be not then alarmed when I tell you that I examined the Devil's pass, went through the Devil's gate, rowed on Satan's stream, and jumped from the Devil's horns.

Life, Letters and Travels of Father Pierre-Jean De Smet, S.J. 1801-1873, edited by Hiram Chittenden and Alfred Richardson, New York: Frances P. Harper, 1905, volume 1.

PREFACE

This book grew out of a Sherman and Mabel Smith Pettyjohn Lecture that I gave at Washington State University. It also is a product of my ongoing interest in artistic and popular images of the American West and of American exploration in a "Second Great Age of Discovery" that spanned the eighteenth and nineteenth centuries. This work focuses especially on pioneer American images of the Pacific Northwest, then known to Americans as "the Oregon Country." There were many images of the Northwest Coast made by oceanic explorers from foreign countries, such as Capt. James Cook and the artists of the Malaspina and Kotzebue expeditions, that I have left out of this book because I was primarily interested in American pioneering images. My intent is to show how the Oregon Country was visualized to potential American settlers, even those in latter days.

Working on this project has been a pleasure. Thanks to the hospitality of Professor David H. Stratton of the History Department at Washington State University and his colleagues, I had a splendid visit to eastern Washington, and a fine audience for my lecture. I must also profusely thank Dr. Fred C. Bohm, of Washington State University Press, whose aid has been invaluable in making this book possible. At one point, also, Suzanne Myklebust was extremely helpful, as was John F. Guido, head of Manuscripts, Archives, and Special Collections at Washington State University Libraries. I must also express my gratitude to the Eastern Washington State Historical Society in Spokane, where I had the pleasure of presenting my Pettyjohn Lecture a second time, and to Professor William Swaggerty and his colleagues at the University of Idaho.

For permission to reprint images from their collections, I wish to thank the following: Library of Congress; U.S. National Gallery of Art; Wisconsin Historical Society; Stark Museum; Royal Ontario Museum; Montreal Museum of Fine Arts; National Gallery of Canada, Ottawa; Yale University Art Gallery and the Beinecke Collection of Western Americana; American Antiquarian Society; Buffalo Bill Historical Center; California State Historical Society; Oregon Historical Society; Provincial Archives of British Columbia at Victoria; Dr. and Mrs. Franz Stenzel; Mr. and Mrs. Edmund Hayes; Dr. D. W. E. Baird;

Columbia River Maritime Museum; Mr. and Mrs. Harold K. Steen; Mrs. Robert Jacroux; Dr. Fred C. Bohm; U.S. National Archives; Washington State Historical Society; Harvard University Library; Sarah Olden Parham; National Geographic Society; Washington State University Libraries; University of Puget Sound Art Department; Eastern Washington State Historical Society; and Amon Carter Museum of American Art.

In addition, I would like to thank Dr. Nancy Anderson of the National Gallery of Art for making prints of George Catlin's Northwest Coast paintings available to me, and for guidance as to the whereabouts of Catlin's "last rambles" in North America. And finally, it is a special pleasure for me to thank my research assistant, Lawrence Walker, and my secretary, Sarah Shelby, to whom this book is dedicated.

William H. Goetzmann
Austin, Texas
1988

INTRODUCTION

In contrast to more traditional views of the American West as a geographical area, William H. Goetzmann has long stressed that the region provided images or projections of futuristic, national wish fulfillment. At various times, Americans have seen the West as the Passage to India, the Great American Desert, a romantic realm of primitivism unspoiled by civilization, a proving ground for Manifest Destiny, a broad stage for the portrayal of dime novel heroes and heroines, the Utopian Garden of Eden for the yeoman farmer, a gigantic laboratory for scientific investigation and experimentation, and so on. Almost forty years ago Henry Nash Smith, in his monumental *Virgin Land: The American West as Symbol and Myth* (1950), emphasized the use of intellectual constructs to interpret the western mystique. From the beginning, Goetzmann's scholarly work also focused on the influence of preconceived eastern ideas, specifically as they affected the explorers, scientists, and artists who conducted reconnaissance in the West. His first book, *Army Exploration in the American West, 1803-1863* (1959), began a trilogy that also included his best-known study, *Exploration and Empire: The Explorer and Scientist in the Winning of the American West* (1966), which was awarded the Pulitzer Prize for American History in 1967. Not surprisingly, both Smith and Goetzmann have played major roles in the development of the interdisciplinary academic approach called American Studies.

Goetzmann's later investigations have followed the exploration theme, as well as branching out into a more direct pursuit of the importance of western art itself. With his son, William N. Goetzmann, he recently authored *The West of the Imagination* (1986), originally intended as a guide for his six-part Public Broadcasting System television series of the same title. Both the series and the book (which took on a life of its own) made significant contributions to an understanding of the mythic West, covering early nineteenth-century art down to modern photography and painting. At the same time Goetzmann wrote the last part of his exploration trilogy, *New Lands, New Men: America and the Second Great Age of Discovery* (1986), which explains the close association of Americans with the spread of a scientific culture around the globe. In this volume he states that it is "the third and final work that I intend to write about Americans and exploration."

The present account, *Looking at the Land of Promise,* is a logical result of Goetzmann's cumulative research. No other part of the United States has been more affected by both exploration and imaginative impressions than the Pacific Northwest. For good or ill, its destiny has always been bound to such expansive concepts as the Northwest Passage to the riches of Asia, the Manifest Destiny of an unfolding America, and an inexhaustible storehouse of natural resources. Reportedly the first European adventurer to see the Northwest coast, Francis Drake, sailed northward until the "stinking fogs" of the region forced him to return to the sunnier latitudes of California. This early image of the Pacific Northwest was also reflected in the writings of explorers and fur traders, who portrayed its coastline as bleak, remote, and storm-wracked. It was viewed as an "American Siberia" with dense forests where, according to the young poet, William Cullen Bryant, a mighty river rolled and heard "no sound/ Save his own dashings. . . ." Only the enthusiastic proclamations of praise sent back East by early American Protestant missionaries, the first white settlers, and later exploring parties changed this negative impression and made the Oregon Country a "corner in the Garden of the World." Goetzmann here depicts this conceptual transformation of the region, drawing on a wealth of understanding about not only western but global exploration and the accompanying visual images as well.

An earlier version of *Looking at the Land of Promise* was presented by William H. Goetzmann when he served as the spring 1984 Pettyjohn Distinguished Lecturer at Washington State University. This lecture series began in the fall of 1980 when the estate of Margaret Pettyjohn provided the university with an endowment designated for the promotion of Pacific Northwest History. These funds established a memorial to her parents, Sherman and Mabel Smith Pettyjohn, pioneers of Walla Walla County. Among the other individuals who gave their generous support to the publication of this book were Lee J. Sahlin of Spokane, President of the Sahlin Foundation; and Stuart B. Bradley of Chicago, McMurray, Black & Snyder, Attorneys at Law. At Washington State University John C. Pierce, Dean of the College of Sciences and Arts, provided advice and support, as did Richard L. Hume, Chair of the Department of History. Several persons at Washington State University Press made substantial contributions of time and expertise: Thomas H. Sanders, Director; Fred C. Bohm, Editor in Chief; Jo Savage, Designer; and Editors Jill Whelchel, Suzanne Myklebust, and Glen Lindeman.

David H. Stratton, Coordinator
Pettyjohn Distinguished Lecture Series
Washington State University
April 1988

LOOKING AT THE LAND OF PROMISE:

PIONEER IMAGES OF THE PACIFIC NORTHWEST

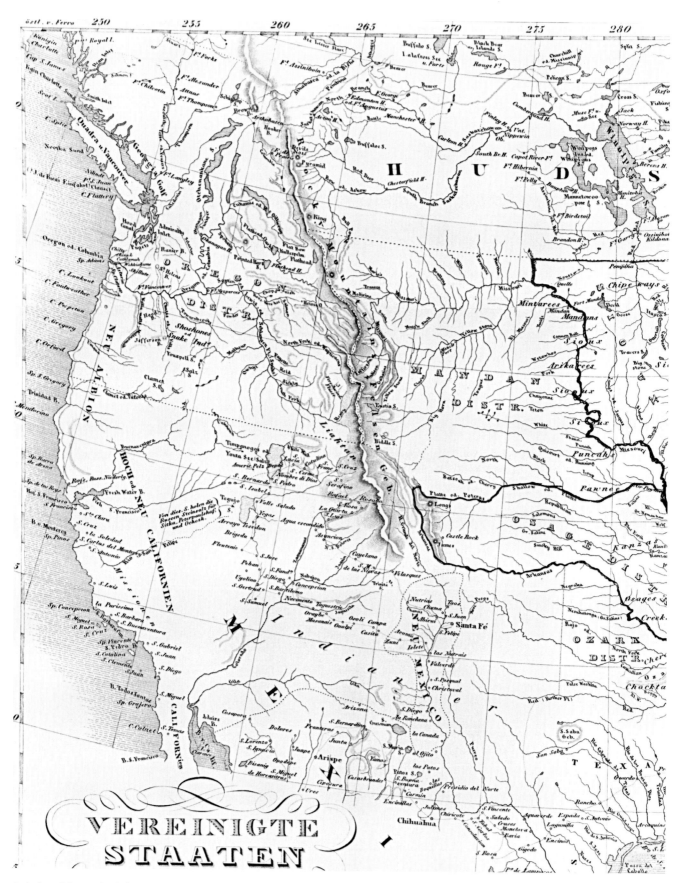

Stieler Map, 1834

Adolf Stieler, *Hand-Atlas über alle Theile der Erde nach dem neuesten Zustande und über das Weltgebäude*, Gotha:
J. Perthes [1837].

$\mathcal{T}$his is a book about information—the kinds of *visual* information available about the Oregon Country, which began in a dream of continental dominance and global imperialism, then became a myth that incorporated plentitude and natural wonders almost beyond belief.

The story begins with visual deprivation and verbal hyperbole. While Thomas Hart Benton,[1] as early as 1819, was calling for "a second Daniel Boone to lead the way" to the Columbia River country, where Americans could "develop its vast means of agriculture and commerce, and . . . open a direct trade between Asia and America . . . ," and Hall Jackson Kelley,[2] in 1831, was extolling the virtues of the incredibly fertile Multnomah Valley where, "The production of vegetables, grain, and cattle, will require . . . but little labor . . . ," few people, especially Benton and Kelley, had any real idea what this promised land looked like.

For most of those heroic argonauts, who filed west over the Oregon Trail in the 1830s, '40s, and even the '50s, the West was a land of hearsay. Information about the West had appeared in the accounts of Lewis and Clark's Expedition[3]

[1] Thomas Hart Benton (1782-1858), the great champion of western expansion, was elected United States Senator from Missouri in 1821, and retained that office for three decades.

[2] An early visionary and propagandist for the acquisition of the Oregon Country, Hall Jackson Kelley (1790-1874) was the person most responsible for informing New Englanders about the Pacific Northwest. He made a career out of promoting the land of his dreams, but only briefly visited it once, in 1832, and was greeted with overt antagonism by the Hudson's Bay Company.

[3] Patrick Gass, *A Journal of the Voyages and Travels of a Corps of Discovery, under the command of Capt. Lewis and Capt. Clarke . . . from the Mouth of the River Missouri through the Interior Parts of North America to the Pacific Ocean, during the years 1804, 1805, & 1806* (Pittsburgh: M'Keehan, 1807); and Nicholas Biddle, ed., *History of the Expedition under the Command of Captains Lewis and Clark, to the Sources of the Missouri, Thence across the Rocky Mountains and down the River Columbia to the Pacific Ocean . . . Prepared for the Press by Paul Allen, Esquire,* 2 vols. (Philadelphia: Bradford & Inskeep, 1814).

and those by Lieutenant Zebulon Pike[4] and Major Stephen H.
Long,[5] as well as descriptions of the Columbia River country
by Gabriel Franchere[6] and Ross Cox,[7] and then the stirring
history of the Astorians' wonderful adventure by Washington
Irving.[8] These were supplemented by a trickle, then a stream,
of mountain men and fur traders' gossip that frequently found

[4] Zebulon Montgomery Pike (1779-1813), leader of the famous expedition to the southern
Rockies in 1806-1807, prepared a poorly organized account of his various western travels
that was published by C. & A. Conrad & Co. of Philadelphia in 1810.

[5] The official report of the 1820 Rocky Mountain exploration led by Stephen H. Long
(1784-1864) was published by the party's physician, Edwin James, in *Account of an Expedition from Pittsburgh to the Rocky Mountains* (1823). Neither Long, nor Pike for
that matter, penetrated as far west as the Oregon Country, but they perpetuated a belief
in a Great American Desert, through which travelers would have to struggle and suffer
to reach the bountiful Pacific Northwest.

[6] Gabriel Franchere (1786-1863) spent the years 1812 to 1814 as a fur trader in the Oregon
Country, first for the American-owned Pacific Fur Company, popularly known as the
Astorians, and later for a short period with Canada's North West Company. He recounted
his adventures in a book published in the French language in Montreal in 1820. An English
translation was not printed until 1854. Two other Astorians, Wilson Price Hunt, chief
agent of the company, and Robert Stuart, the explorer of the Oregon Trail, also wrote
an account in French in Paris in 1821. This important work was not published in English until 1935.

[7] Beginning in 1812, Ross Cox (1793-1853) spent six years as a fur trader in the Oregon
Country, first with the Astorians and later the North West Company. Returning to his
Irish homeland, he eventually wrote an account of his experiences titled *Adventures
on the Columbia River* (London, 1831), which was immensely popular in both Great
Britain and America.

[8] Washington Irving (1783-1859), America's literary genius who created stories about
Ichabod Crane and Rip Van Winkle, also wrote on historical subjects in Europe's Iberian
Peninsula and in the New World. Eventually turning his attention to the West, Irving
authored, among other works, the incomparable *Astoria, or Anecdotes of an Enterprise
beyond the Rocky Mountains* in 1836. This account told the story of the visionary Astorian
venture, which had been an attempt to develop the fur trade on a continental basis with
the Oregon Country as the focal point. From 1811 to 1813, the far-ranging Astorians
nearly succeeded, but finally were defeated by complications arising from logistical prob-
lems and the War of 1812, after which Canadian fur hunters dominated the Oregon Country. *Astoria* was written at the request of Irving's good friend, John Jacob Astor. A resi-
dent of New York, Astor was the organizer of the great fur trade scheme, and, despite
its failure, he eventually became the wealthiest man in the nation through realty in-
vestments as well as commercial and fur trade dealings.

its way into the nation's newspapers.[9] Then, in 1845, Lieutenant John Charles Frémont published his climactic and dramatic account of his survey of the entire West in 1843-1844. This proved to be inspirational, and helped launch a second wave of emigrants, who followed in the wake of those first brave souls and soul-savers who had made their way to Oregon in the 1830s and early 1840s. None of the accounts mentioned above, however, really pictured the Far West in anything except the most rudimentary terms. The few works by Samuel Seymour in Long's "Report," the truly bizarre woodcuts accompanying Sergeant Patrick Gass's Lewis and Clark Expedition "Journal," Charles Preuss's very limited lithographs in Frémont's "Report," and the illustrations in Lieutenant Charles Wilkes's "Report" on the great United States Exploring Expedition[10] as it touched Oregon and California, constituted about all the pictorial data available to the American people during the onset of one of the greatest mass migrations in human history.

Alfred Jacob Miller, who had painted the mountain men frolicking in the heart of the Rocky Mountains in 1837, had taken his wonderful watercolors to Murthly Castle in

[9] Also during the latter part of this period, scientists, missionaries, and other adventurous Oregon Country travelers increasingly wrote accounts in magazines, newspapers, official reports, and even a few books. Among the more prominent and best known works were those by the Reverend Samuel Parker in 1838, botanist John Kirk Townsend in 1839, and Oregon enthusiast Thomas Jefferson Farnham in 1841. Missionaries, in particular, actively disseminated information in Europe and America. For example, the famous Belgian priest, Pierre De Smet (1801-1873), wrote prolifically in six languages about his travels and proselytizing in the Oregon Country and the northern Rockies.

[10] Charles Wilkes (1798-1877), of the United States Navy, led a flotilla on a worldwide expedition in the years 1838-1842. After confirming that Antarctica was a continent and charting much of the south and central Pacific, the explorers sailed to the Oregon Country in 1841. Upon their arrival, contingents of sailors, marines, scientists, and artists investigated both coastal and inland areas. In 1844-1845, Wilkes published a *Narrative of the United States Exploring Expedition*. In 1861 during the Civil War, Wilkes gained international notoriety by illegally seizing two Confederate diplomatic agents from the British steamer *Trent*, while on the high seas of the Atlantic.

Scotland, and George Catlin had taken his Missouri River works to London and Paris, where they were more appreciated than in Jacksonian Washington. Later, in 1855, on one of his incredible "last rambles" from Tierra del Fuego to Alaska, Catlin stopped at Vancouver Island to paint the Klahoquat Indians attacking a beached whale and the Nayas carving a war canoe deep in the forest. The American public did not see these Catlin paintings until they were displayed at the Smithsonian in 1871, the year before Catlin died. And, except for a small, short-lived Paris exhibition, no one saw Karl Bodmer's magnificent watercolors until Prince Maximilian's "Atlas" with eighty-two stunning aquatints was published in 1841 in Paris; and then few could afford to purchase it.[11] Thus, when the Oregon and California trails opened up, the Far West was, comparatively speaking, a visual unknown, or more accurately, a visual abstraction.

The Far West was a visual abstraction because it was largely pictured on maps which are abstract collections of signs that, correctly understood, constitute a picture of a part of the earth. Due to the intense competition for the fur trade of the Northwest Coast and a continual search for a Northwest Passage, beginning in the late eighteenth century, maps of the Pacific Northwest abounded, including those made by such early seagoing visitors as captains James Cook, George Vancouver,

[11] Each of the artists, Alfred Jacob Miller (1810-1874), George Catlin (1796-1872), and Karl Bodmer (1809-1893), journeyed to the western Great Plains or up the Missouri River in the 1830s, making an outstanding record of the landscape and Indian and white inhabitants. Their paintings were well received in the East and especially Europe. In addition, the paintings helped to dispel the myth of a Great American Desert barring the way to Oregon—a misconception openly challenged by John Charles Frémont's 1845 report.

In 1855 George Catlin arrived by ship in the Oregon Country and what is now British Columbia. He made numerous paintings of Northwest Coast Indians and then turned eastward and crossed the West from the Northwest to the mouth of the Rio Grande. See George Catlin, *Episodes from "Life Among the Indians" and "Last Rambles,"* Marvin C. Ross, ed., reprint edition (Norman: University of Oklahoma Press, 1979).

4

Bruno Hezeta, and Alejandro Malaspina.[12] The oceanic maps do tell a story—the story of imperialism and global geopolitics aimed primarily at control of the North Pacific and the China trade.

But the maps of the interior of the Northwest country tell a story as well. Lewis and Clark's great manuscript map of 1809 (see pg. 6), on view in Clark's office in St. Louis, revealed the whole complex geography of the Northwest for the first time. Clark constantly updated it with information from explorers, mountain men, fur traders, and Indian friends. The excellent version of this map that appeared with Biddle and Allen's widely-distributed, semiofficial account of Lewis and Clark's expedition in 1814, pictured the Northwest country and the strategic Columbia River to a larger public audience (see pg. 7).

The work of the master cartographer/explorer of the region, the Canadian, David Thompson,[13] was not widely distributed. But even the North West Company, and later the Hudson's Bay Company, could not keep a secret forever, and his work formed the basis for Aaron Arrowsmith's masterful maps coming out of London. As early as 1821, Chevalier Lapie incorporated data from Lewis and Clark, David Thompson,

[12] James Cook (1728-1779) and George Vancouver (1758-1798) guided English expeditions, whereas Bruno Hezeta (1771-1807) and Alejandro Malaspina (1754-1810) represented Spain. By the late eighteenth century, Spanish, British, American, Russian, French, and Portuguese sailors had confirmed that no seaway, i.e., a Northwest Passage of myth and legend, connected Hudson's Bay with the Pacific Ocean and the rich commerce of the Orient.

[13] Welsh-born David Thompson (1770-1857) left the Hudson's Bay Company in 1797 to work for the North West Company. Employed primarily as a surveyor or "astronomer," Thompson investigated and charted new lands for exploitation by his fur trading comrades. It was in this capacity that he entered the Oregon Country early in the nineteenth century, establishing the first trading posts in present-day Idaho and western Montana. He left the region in 1812, never to return. His reputation as a pioneer geographer of the inland Pacific Northwest is equaled by few, including Lewis and Clark.

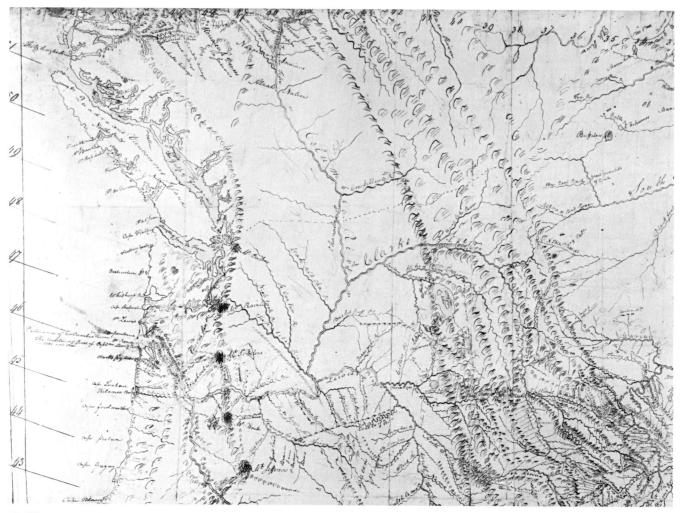

William Clark Map, circa 1809-1810

Reprint from Beinecke Library, Yale University, New Haven, Connecticut

The Lewis and Clark expedition left the St. Louis vicinity on May 14, 1804, and proceeded via the Missouri and Columbia watersheds to the Pacific Ocean, which they reached in the autumn of 1805. Captain Meriwether Lewis (1774-1809), of the First United States Infantry Regiment, previously had served as Thomas Jefferson's private secretary and was hand-picked by the President to head the exploration. After completing further investigations in the vast, largely unknown West, they arrived back in St. Louis on September 23, 1806. Having been given up for dead by almost everyone except Jefferson, the explorers were greeted with much celebrating. In 28 months, the party's several dozen members had traveled more than 8,000 miles. They were the first white men to cross the North American continent between the Spanish provinces of California and New Mexico and the British-controlled lands to the north.

William Clark (1770-1838), a long-time friend of Meriwether Lewis, had served as coleader of the Corps of Discovery. The talents and temperaments of the two able commanders were superbly complementary—Lewis was well trained scientifically and was more literate, whereas Clark was adept at Indian negotiations and served as the principal navigator and mapmaker. As a reward for the successful completion of the expedition, President Jefferson in 1807 appointed Clark as Indian agent of Louisiana Territory and brigadier general of the militia.

Clark drew a great map of the West, relying on Indian sketches, his own firsthand observations, the works of other explorers, and information from other western adventurers, primarily fur hunters who had followed in the wake of the Corps of Discovery and now were returning to St. Louis, the main gateway to the West. In about 1810, Clark sent this map, or more probably one similar to it, to Philadelphia to be used in preparing the map published in the 1814 official history of the Lewis and Clark expedition. For reasons not clearly understood, the makers of the engraved map altered or changed some aspects of Clark's geography. Consequently, the official, engraved map was not as reliable as Clark's original, which soon disappeared and was only rediscovered in the 1950s, in an old desk in St. Paul, Minnesota.

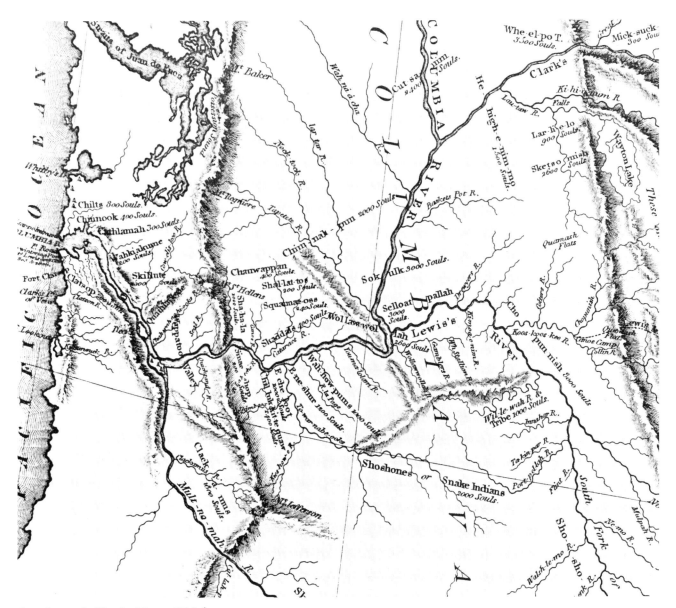

Lewis and Clark Map, 1814

Library of Congress, Washington, D.C.

Lewis and Clark's Corps of Discovery had returned from the Far West in 1806, but an official history and map of the expedition was not published until eight years later due to various delays, not the least of which was Meriwether Lewis's untimely death in 1809. By February 1814, the long awaited History of the Expedition Under the Command of Captains Lewis and Clark *was finally finished by editors Nicholas Biddle and Paul Allen.*

When at length it came out with its beautifully engraved map "copied by Samuel Lewis from the original drawing by William Clark," the work at once took its place as a classic in the literature of discovery and exploration.

One of the first cartographic results of the trip was the enforced recognition by everyone that the North American continent was much wider than had been thought, or, if not wider, then the Missouri [River] ended far short of the Pacific. Indeed, instead of rising in mountains quite near the western seaboard, the Missouri (long though it be) originated far—very far indeed—from the mouth of the Columbia. Full appreciation . . . of the "River of the West" was also a major result of Lewis and Clark's exploration. Until they—and shortly later the North West Company's fur traders—actually traversed the Columbia's tremendous watershed, few had realized either its extent or its grandeur, even though the magic words "Oregon" and "River of the West" had at times been applied to it. Moreover, Lewis and Clark's exploration and the resulting map in time were to become among the prime foundation stones on which American claim to Oregon was erected.

Carl I. Wheat, *Mapping the Transmississippi West, 1540-1861*, vol. 2, 1958, pp. 31-32.

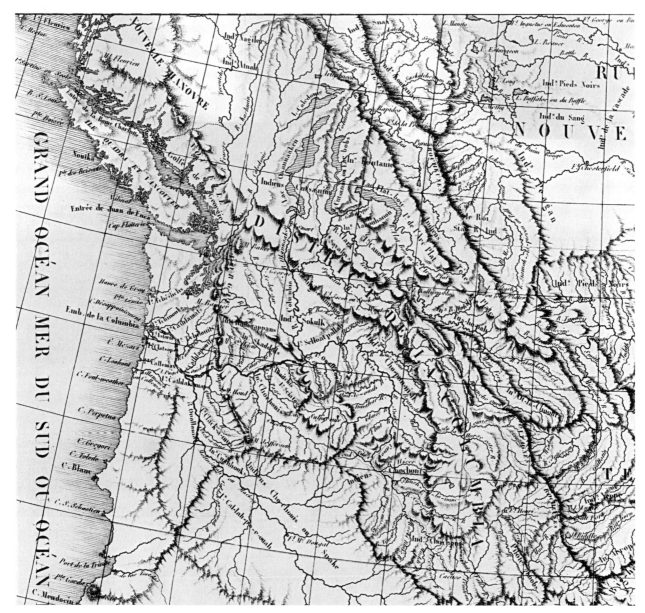

Chevalier Lapie Map, 1821
Library of Congress, Washington, D.C.

This map, prepared by a French cartographer, Chevalier Lapie, was published with the Wilson Price Hunt and Robert Stuart journals in Nouvelles Annales des Voyages, *Tomes 10 and 12, in Paris in 1821. European mapmakers retained a great interest in the geography of western North America and tried to incorporate the latest discoveries in their works. Lapie's chart was based mainly on the pivotal Lewis and Clark map of 1814, but also included new information provided by the far-ranging Astorians as well as by the intrepid British fur traders from Canada. Particularly noteworthy are Stuart's location of the south pass of the Rocky Mountains and the much improved depictions of the upper Columbia and Snake river watersheds—the result of thorough investigations by fur hunters in the 1810s. Lapie's map retained the erroneous belief that the Multnomah River (now the Willamette River of western Oregon) extended far into the interior of the continent, nearly to what is now northwest Utah.*

A contemporary, Hudson's Bay Company governor George Simpson, testified to the inaccuracy of these early maps in his journal: "I have examined with much attention the different charts and maps that have appeared of this Country but none of them have any thing like a correct idea thereof, Rivers, Lakes, Mountains, Plains, & Forests being introduced and disposed as suited the fancy and taste of the Draftsmen and some of the writers have had the effrontery to Gull the public with the produce of their own fertile imaginations differing widely from the truth and with descriptions of Countries they have never seen and which had not been explored when their works came from the Press."

George Simpson's *Journal,* 1824-1825, edited by Frederick Merk, Harvard University Press, 1931.

and the Astorians in a map published in the French series *Nouvelles Annales des Voyages*[14] (see pg. 8).

A. H. Brué, geographer to the King of France, also published important maps of North America based on this data. And the enterprising Philadelphian, Henry Schenck Tanner, in his *New American Atlas* of 1822 (see pg. 10), produced what Carl I. Wheat[15] called a "monumental" map, a "landmark," even a "great cartographical achievement" with his map of the American West just after the conclusion of the Adams-Onis, or Transcontinental Boundary Treaty, between the United States and Spain in 1819. In showing the boundary as it traced across the West of the continent to the Pacific, Tanner was pointing out America's first clearly recognized "window on the Pacific." The map also indicated the new limits of the Spanish and Russian territories in North America, and the British-American occupation zone stemming from the joint occupation agreement of 1818.[16]

[14] Lapie's map was a supplement in the 1821 French-language publication of the journals of the two prominent Astorians, Wilson Price Hunt and David Stuart. The French had a keen interest in the exploration of unknown lands, as is demonstrated by the fact that the *Nouvelles Annales de Voyages* series eventually included 212 volumes about geographical discovery.

[15] Carl I. Wheat (b. 1892), the West's preeminent cartographic scholar, is the author of *Mapping the Transmississippi West*, 6 vols. (San Francisco: Institute of Historical Cartography, 1957-1963).

[16] The boundaries of the Oregon Country were defined by the Convention of 1818, the Adams-Onis Treaty of 1819, and diplomatic agreements with Russia in the early 1820s. Thus by the mid-1820s, Spanish and Russian claims were eliminated, and the United States and Great Britain agreed to jointly occupy the region—an arrangement that held for another two decades. The Oregon Country included all of the territory lying west of the Rocky Mountain Continental Divide, between the 42nd parallel on the south, which is the present southern boundary of the states of Oregon and Idaho, and 54 degrees 40 minutes north latitude in what is now British Columbia. All of present-day Washington, Idaho, and Oregon were included, as well as parts of western Montana and Wyoming and about half of British Columbia. In 1846, Great Britain and the United States finally divided up this vast area by establishing the international boundary at the 49th parallel.

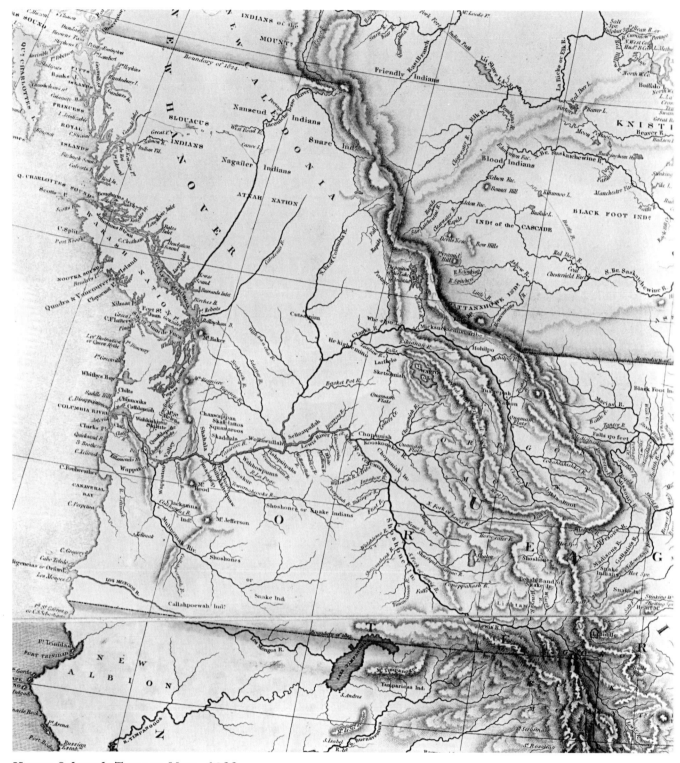

Henry Schenck Tanner Map, 1822
Library of Congress, Washington, D.C.

Master engraver Henry Schenck Tanner (1786-1858) of Philadelphia produced this map in 1822 with an official endorsement from the United States "Dept. of State." Tanner had no access to the detailed information that the Astorians could have provided, and consequently his depiction of the Pacific Northwest was little improved over that of the 1814 Lewis and Clark map. His chart, however, successfully upgraded information about other regions of the Far West. It became the progenitor of a long series of maps utilized by the American public throughout the 1820s. By the end of the decade, Tanner's maps finally incorporated information from the fur trade explorers about the region which just then was becoming known as "Oregon."

British North America by Aaron Arrowsmith, 1834

Library of Congress, Washington, D.C.

Aaron Arrowsmith had access to geographic information collected by the Hudson's Bay Company and other British fur traders, namely David Thompson, Alexander Ross, William Kittson, and Peter Skene Ogden.

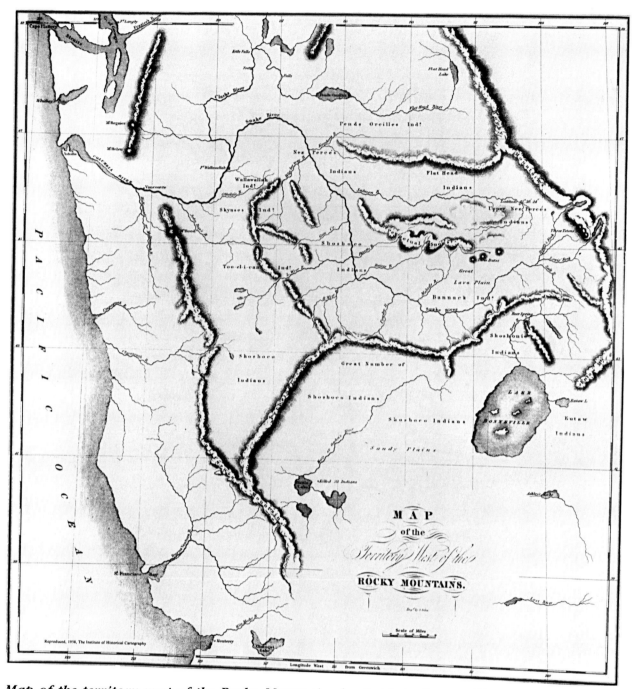

Map of the territory west of the Rocky Mountains by Captain Bonneville, 1837
Carl I. Wheat, *Mapping the Transmississippi West*, San Francisco, California

This map appeared in Washington Irving's book, The Adventures of Captain Bonneville, *1837.*

All of Tanner's subsequent maps of the region made "territorial imperative" points, as did Aaron Arrowsmith's important map of 1834 (see pg. 11), based not only on David Thompson's work, but also nearly three decades of Canadian fur trade brigade forays into the Pacific Northwest. Throughout the 1830s, French and German mapmakers generally took their cue from Arrowsmith and son. Stieler's German map of 1834 (see pg. xxii) is an example of this.

Meantime, one must not overlook American propaganda maps. Captain Benjamin Bonneville's important map of 1837 (see pg. 12) represents the fanciful vision of an American spy sent to counter the British by President Jackson himself.[17] Hall Jackson Kelley's map of 1839 may well be considered a utopian blueprint for the Northwest by that consummate

---

[17] A French immigrant and graduate of West Point, Benjamin Louis Eulalie de Bonneville (1796-1878) was a soldier, fur hunter, and explorer in the West. In 1832-1835, while on leave from the U.S. Army, he led a fur trading enterprise that competed unsuccessfully against the established American and British firms already in the Rockies and Oregon. Shortly after returning to the East, Bonneville's experiences were immortalized when Washington Irving wrote *The Adventures of Captain Bonneville* in 1837, based on interviews and written narratives from the Army captain. Speculation has arisen over whether or not President Andrew Jackson specifically ordered Bonneville to scrutinize British activities in the Oregon Country. The truth of this matter remains unknown. It is an acknowledged fact, however, that officers on long-term leave, who were travelling or conducting personal business in the West, or in other parts of the world for that matter, were expected on their return to give full reports of their observations to the Departments of War or State.

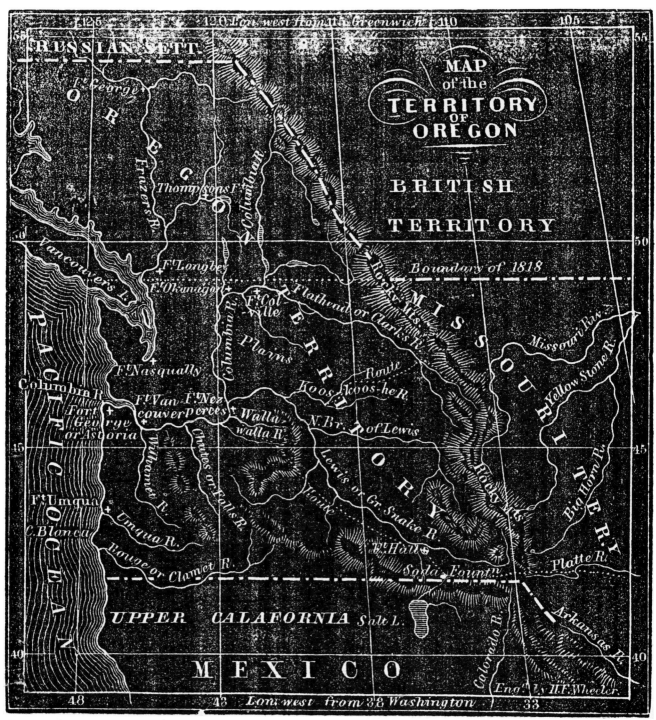

Oregon Territory

From the *Ohio Statesman,* August 28, 1844

State Historical Society of Wisconsin, Madison, Wisconsin

14

emigrant propagandist. But the work of H. F. Wheeler, appearing in the *Weekly Ohio Statesman* for Aug. 28, 1844, looked even more like a blueprint for conquest (see pg. 14). This newspaper, popularly known as "the Ohio Coon Catcher," castigated Henry Clay and John Quincy Adams[18] for losing American soil in the Northwest, since they had officially expressed a willingness to divide up the Oregon Country with the British. The entire region, the paper pointed out, was equal in area to the original thirteen states. The white-on-black format of the map was a real attention getter, as its funereal appearance offered an eloquent lament for Clay's folly, and the editor accompanied the map-picture with choice Manifest Destiny comments, like "Oregon is ours! let us not elect a party to power that will forever give it, or a part of it, to the enemy."[19]

The climactic and authoritative American maps of the region, however, were those drawn by Lieutenant Wilkes and his staff in 1841 and published in 1844, together with the maps drawn by Lieutenant John Charles Frémont and his German cartographer, Charles Preuss, and published in 1848.

[18] John Quincy Adams was the sixth President of the United States, serving in 1825-1829. The noted statesman, Henry Clay, had been instrumental in getting Adams elected, and, in recognition of that fact, Adams appointed Clay as Secretary of State. Cries of corruption immediately arose from opposition elements, and continued to be brought against Clay throughout his long and illustrious career in government. The Adams administration's policy in regard to the Oregon Question was basically that both Great Britain and the United States had legitimate claims and the 49th parallel should be the dividing line between British and American sectors. This essentially came to pass years later in the 1846 Oregon Treaty worked out during the Polk presidency.

[19] "The Ohio Coon Catcher" sided with some vociferous elements in the Democratic party calling for annexation of all of the Oregon Country and, of course, complete expulsion of the British. These Democrats detested Whig politicians, such as Clay and Adams, who were willing to compromise with the British on this issue. Ironically, it was a Democratic administration that finally signed an agreement with the English to divide up the Oregon Country.

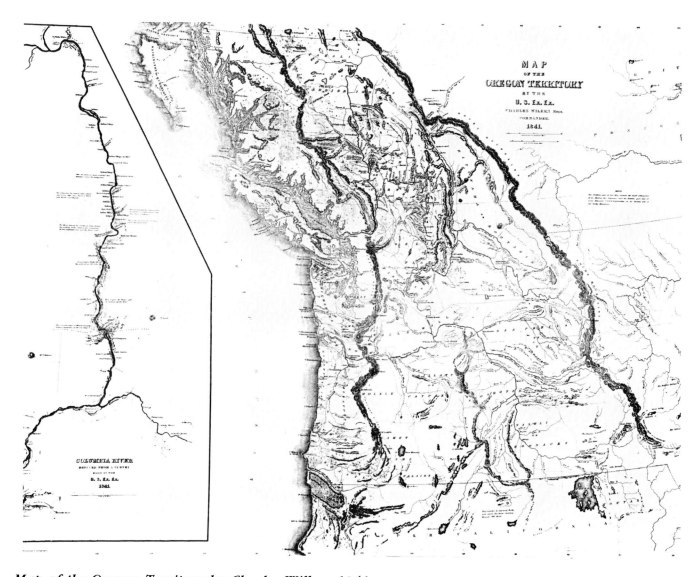

Map of the Oregon Territory by Charles Wilkes, 1841

Carl I. Wheat, *Mapping the Transmississippi West,* San Francisco, California

Wilkes's very scientific maps (see pg. 16) pictured the whole rich, complex Columbia and Willamette country, and his report stressed the importance of Puget Sound, mapped by him in detail, as the only feasible place for an American Pacific Northwest port. Frémont's map (see pg. 18) proved that no river ran west from the Great Salt Lake, and also stressed the importance of the Oregon Country, as well as California. Preuss's emigrant map, in seven detailed sections, formed the most important practical guide to Oregon and California. It proved to be a far more accurate picture of the West than Lansford W. Hastings's *The Emigrants' Guide to Oregon and California* of 1845,[20] which helped to get the Donner Party into so much tragic difficulty as many in the party perished trying to cross California's snowy Sierras.[21]

However revealing the story they tell, maps were an abstract view of the great Northwest. They could never really

[20] Lansford Warren Hastings (1818?-1868) and Elijah White led the first wagon train of immigrants to Oregon in 1842. Hastings played a conspicuous role in politics and law in Oregon and especially California. In 1845, he wrote the controversial and somewhat irresponsible guidebook, which led the Donner Party to their infamous destiny. During the Civil War, he concocted an elaborate, and ultimately unsuccessful, plan to capture California and the Southwest for the Confederacy. After the war, he started a colony in Brazil for recalcitrant Rebels, and died at sea when returning to Alabama for more emigrants.

[21] Throughout the winter of 1846-1847, the ill-fated Donner wagon train remained trapped in the snowy Sierra Nevada range of California. Experiencing hunger, exposure, and ultimately cannibalism, only 45 of the 89 immigrants lived to reach the settlements of the Sacramento Valley.

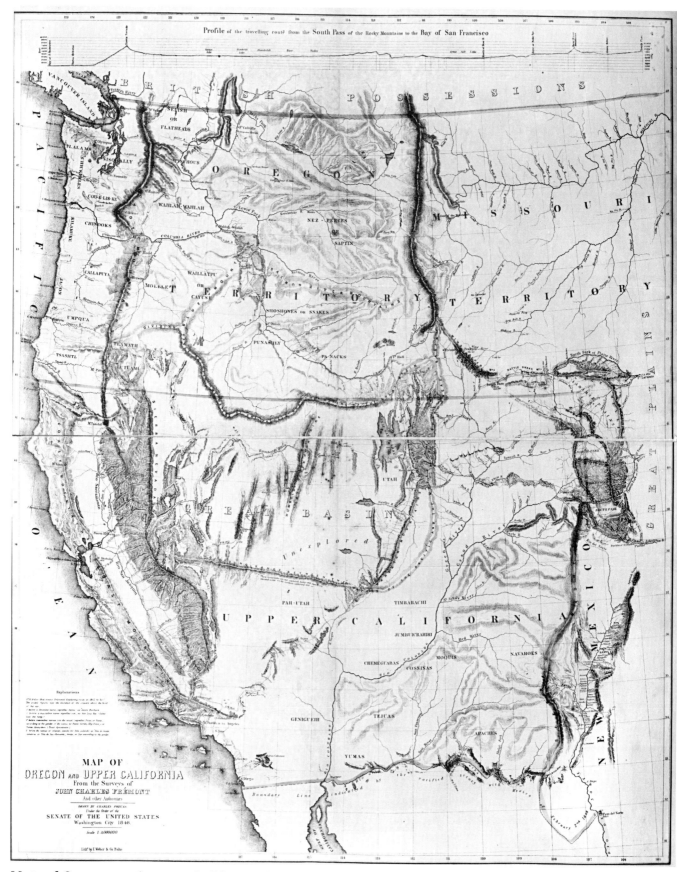

Map of Oregon and upper California by John Charles Frémont, 1848

Library of Congress, Washington, D.C.

portray nature's grandeur, plentitude, or its difficulties. They also could not portray the human factor—the mysterious Indian tribes with their exotic rituals and even more exotic art that anticipated cubism by perhaps 1000 years, and the Euro-American pioneers just then "coming into the country." It took artists and photographers to do that.

Some of the artists came by sea—with Great Britain's Cook and Vancouver expeditions of the late eighteenth century. Cook's artists in particular were masters of the dramatic, but Vancouver's men had their moments too.[22]

The first "American" artists of any consequence to portray the great Northwest came with Lieutenant Wilkes on the United States Exploring Expedition in 1841. They were Alfred T. Agate and Joseph Drayton, by then veterans of Wilkes's cruise to the icy reaches of the Antarctic and through hundreds of remote South Sea Islands. One of Wilkes's major

[22] Northwest art done by the Spanish in the late eighteenth century was of exceptionally high quality, but, of course, it remained in Mexico and Spain and was unknown in the United States.

Wreck of the Peacock by Alfred T. Agate
Beinecke Library, Yale University, New Haven, Connecticut

Agate's depiction of the sinking of the Peacock *when it tried to enter the mouth of the Columbia, July 18, 1841. All men on board were saved.*

Alfred Agate worked as an artist in New York City from 1831-1838, where he trained under Professor Thomas Cummings. In 1838, Agate joined Charles Wilkes in the around-the-world United States Exploring Expedition; he and fellow artist Joseph Drayton were part of the corps of scientists attached to the expedition. In 1842, Agate returned to Washington, D.C., to prepare his sketches and paintings for publication. His work is reproduced in Wilkes's five-volume narrative report, The United States Exploring Expedition, *published in 1844.*

ships, the *Peacock*, was wrecked on the bar off the mouth of the Columbia River. Agate managed to portray this sad event (see pg. 20), and his picture, as it appeared in Wilkes's report, had real meaning because it, more than a thousand words, demonstrated that the Columbia River estuary provided no satisfactory harbor, and that American policy makers had better aim at acquiring the Puget Sound area. Agate also sketched Astoria, thus providing a pictorial documentation of one of America's chief claims to the Columbia River region[23]—this despite the fact that Astoria had long since come under the domination of hardy Canadian voyageurs, and Fort William, as it was renamed, was regularly visited by the Hudson's Bay Company's *Beaver*, the first steamboat to ply the waters of the Pacific Northwest. No artist, however, had yet depicted the hardy American pioneers struggling into Oregon's promised lands by all manner of conveyance.

[23] American claims to the Oregon Country were based mainly on Captain Robert Gray's discovery of the mouth of the Columbia in 1792, Lewis and Clark's exploration of 1805-1806, and the establishment of Fort Astoria by the ill-fated Pacific Fur Company in 1811. Great Britain countered with Cook and Vancouver's coastal investigations of 1778 and 1792, Alexander Mackenzie's and Simon Fraser's more northerly overland expeditions to the sea in 1793 and 1808, and years of occupation by Canadian fur trading communities.

Some of the earliest drawings of Pacific Northwest scenes were by Father Nicholas Point, an associate of the great Jesuit missionary Pierre De Smet. Point drew views of the Catholic missions in the interior, including *St. Mary's among the Flatheads* (in present-day western Montana), which made it appear as if the Holy Ghost had indeed descended upon the Oregon Country (shown above). He also made a drawing of an ideal Jesuit town plan whose semicircular design resembled the ground plan of the Anasazi ruins in Chaco Canyon, New Mexico (see pg. 23). Point's drawings of missions, Indians, and utopian towns, as well as racy action views, became the illustrations for De Smet's classic book, *Oregon Missions and Travels Over the Rocky Mountains in 1845-46* (1847).

Among the first important renditions of the Oregon Country by a professional artist were those of Paul Kane, from sketches made in 1846 and 1847. Kane, born in Ireland, was raised in York, now Toronto, Canada. He studied with Thomas Drury, Canada's foremost art teacher, with the practical intention of being a portrait painter. Instead, Kane began his career as a painter of signs and furniture. Ultimately, he moved to Detroit, then traveled down the Mississippi to New Orleans and Mobile, Alabama. In Mobile, he enjoyed his greatest financial success as a portrait painter. This enabled him to journey to Italy to study the Old Masters. The turning

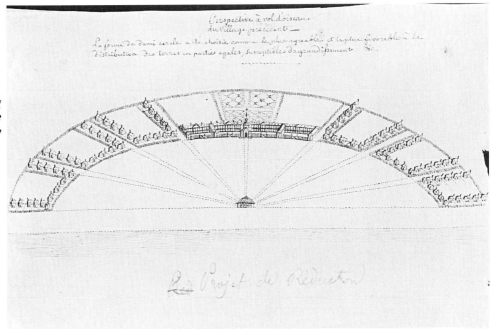

point in Kane's life, however, came when he met George Catlin in England in 1843. Observing Catlin's success with his Indian Gallery, and absorbing Catlin's enthusiasm for the "vanishing race," Kane determined to return home and do the same for the Indians of lower Canada. He returned to Mobile, where he paused for two years to accumulate funds for his proposed western journey, and in 1845 he set out west across Canada on a painting mission that lasted three years.

In crossing western Canada, Kane traveled with Hudson's Bay Company brigades, stopping at the Company's forts or houses, which he painted to form an important historical record. By December of 1846, Kane had crossed the great western prairies, the Canadian Rockies, and descended the Columbia to Fort Vancouver, then in charge of the veteran fur hunter, Peter Skene Ogden.[24] In 1847, Kane traveled over much of the Oregon Territory, hurriedly attempting to portray its Indians and its pristine scenery on canvas before the American invasion spoiled it forever. His anxiety in this matter is reflected in a list of American immigrants that he compiled: five American settlers had arrived in 1834; by 1844, the number had reached 1,475; then 3,000 in 1845; and 7,000 to

[24] As a brigade leader for the Hudson's Bay Company in the 1820s and early 1830s, Peter Skene Ogden (1794-1854) investigated and exploited a vast portion of the West, including the Snake River plains, eastern Oregon, the Great Salt Lake, the Great Basin, and northern California. He later was in charge of trading posts in the northern part of the Oregon Country, before becoming "chief factor" at Fort Vancouver. Wealthy in his retirement years, this great explorer of the fur trade era traveled to the East and Europe, but preferred to live in the West, where he died at Oregon City in 1854.

Breakfast July 19, 1845, Rocky Mountains by Henry James Warre
American Antiquarian Society, Worcester, Massachusetts

. . . The night was very cold & on the morning of Saturday 19th we found the whole ground covered with a thick White Frost which was followed by a lovely day.—off at 5 oC through the same kind of thick wood & over swamp, till 11 oC when we reached a chain of very high hills and a much clearer & more practicable country—with beautiful views on all sides, of the distant Prairies—Passing over this range we came to a second, on surmounting which we came in sight of the magnificent Range of the Rocky Mountains, formed in all the irregularity of Mountain Scenery and stretching far away into the blue distance North & South. From the height of the Hills on which we stood the intervening country appeared like an extensive plain, and made the Mountains appear very large; Snow covered several, and had accumulated in the Valleys; but I was disappointed at seeing so little—nor will the Rocky Mountains bear comparison with the Alps either in size or magnificence of outline—Had I not seen Switzerland I should have been much more struck, but I had allowed my imagination too much scope & as is frequently the case, I was on the whole disappointed.—We breakfasted in full view of the Mountains and descended afterwards to an immense plain, which proved to be an deep swamp— through which we were obliged to pass to a River called by Indians Medicine Lodge River—. . .

From Warre's *Journal,* vol. 1, pp. 1035-1037.

8,000 in 1846, just before his arrival. The Oregon Treaty, declaring American sovereignty over all the territory south of the 49th parallel (excluding the southern tip of Vancouver Island), had been signed in 1846, and by the time Kane reached Fort Vancouver, the Hudson's Bay Company was pulling back to Victoria on Vancouver Island.[25] The year before Kane arrived, the British spy, Captain Henry Warre, had come into the country sketching and taking notes as to the feasibility of a British stand before the American advance. Warre's sketches were widely distributed as lithographs (see pp. 60-63), and thus preceded Kane's work.

Kane knew that others, such as Catlin, had painted the Plains Indians, but few had captured the fierce Northwest Coast people on canvas, so he concentrated a great deal of his efforts on those Indians, as well as on the Columbia Plateau tribes of the interior—the Nez Perce, Flathead, Cayuse, and the Umatilla. Elements of the Cayuse band, feeling pressure from American settlers invading their lands, rose up to massacre Marcus Whitman[26] just as Kane approached Whitman's Waiilatpu mission. Kane had arrived at a dramatic moment in Northwest history—a moment that he recorded not

[25] It can be assumed that Kane, a British subject, did not look favorably on the growing American migration to the Pacific Northwest, nor the Hudson's Bay Company's forced withdrawal from its forts located in what is today Washington, Oregon, and Idaho. By this time the fur trade was declining, though the Hudson's Bay Company would continue to remain active in British Columbia and elsewhere in Canada.

[26] In November 1847, Marcus Whitman (1802-1847), his wife Narcissa, and twelve others died in the famous attack on the Waiilatpu mission near present-day Walla Walla, Washington.

only in his paintings, but in a stirring book which he published in 1859, *Wanderings of an Artist Among the Indians of North America From Canada to Vancouver's Island and Oregon through the Hudson's Bay Company's Territory and Back Again.*[27] The manuscript of this work, written in his wife's hand, now resides at the Stark Museum in Orange, Texas, together with the major collection of Kane's paintings.

J. Russell Harper, in *Paul Kane's Frontier* (1971), has long since presented a definitive review of Kane's work, but it is important for our purposes to see it in three broad aspects: Indian portraits (of which he made a great many), the careful documentation of Indian artifacts and customs, and the rendition of the far western landscape. In all three aspects Kane excelled. The first two genres fall into the category of ethnological art, which for many years has been the province of anthropologists who have failed to see not only its aesthetic merits, but the romantic spirit behind the work that gave the artist the impulse to venture out into the wilderness to make such drawings and paintings in the first place.

Only now are we beginning to see his work as an example of the great era of European and American romantic science. Kane's works in this genre, rivaled only by those of the Swiss, Karl Bodmer, and perhaps George Catlin, are prime examples of this impulse and this mind-set. He was stunned by the exotic, mysterious, original peoples of the Northwest. And if he was as credulous as Lewis and Clark regarding head-flattening and other "customs," his wide-eyed, naive curiosity about Indian ceremonies and his astonished admiration for

---

[27] Kane sketched and painted Indians in a decidedly positive and idealistic manner, therefore it is somewhat surprising to find in *Wanderings of an Artist* that he wrote many critical, if not outright chauvinistic, remarks about Native Americans and their culture.

their elaborate, often indecipherable artifacts shows through in his paintings and drawings. They constantly reflect wonder and mystery and a feeling for the exotic. On the one hand, fierce dancers in raven transformation masks excite that most cherished of romantic emotions, terror, while, on the other hand, the forlorn female village totem statue seems to evoke that other set of cherished romantic emotions, pity, and lament for vanished civilizations. The village totem figure is Paul Kane's equivalent of Shelley's celebrated "Ozymandias."[28]

Kane also painted the natural wonders of the Northwest, thereby starting what has remained perhaps the primary tradition in the art and photography of the region. With towering mountains, great gorges, dense forests of huge trees, and roaring streams dominating the region, one could hardly ignore the unmatched opportunities for landscape painting. Few areas in the world could match it for contrast and variety, and hence, novelty. Kane's most famous effort at capturing this novelty were his renditions of Mt. St. Helens erupting in 1847. He painted at least three versions of this—a wispy eruption in broad daylight, a dramatic dawn eruption, complete with mushroom cloud, and a lurid night scene that looked like a Roman candle fireworks display. Clearly he

[28] I met a traveler from an antique land [Egypt],
Who said: Two vast and trunkless legs of stone
Stand in the desert. Near them, on the sand,
Half sunk, a shattered visage lies. . . .
And on the pedestal these words appear:
 "My name is Ozymandias, King of Kings:
Look on my works, ye Mighty, and despair!"
Nothing beside remains. Round the decay
Of that colossal wreck, boundless and bare
The lone and level sands stretch far away.

Percy Bysshe Shelley (1792-1822)

Oregon City on the Willamette River by John Mix Stanley
Amon Carter Museum, Fort Worth, Texas

Oregon City was an early focal point of settlement in the Oregon Country. It was an important transportation center and a natural place for early travelers to stop. Stanley's painting renders it as a symbol of prosperous, peaceful settlement in Oregon.

linked the volcano's eruption with the other ethnographic mysteries he had observed. Were the earth gods angry with the invaders of the Northwest country who built "progressive" towns like Oregon City on the Willamette?

While Kane could be mystical, Captain Henry Warre matter-of-factly recorded Oregon City as one more instance of inevitable American encroachment, and John Mix Stanley, in a beautiful work executed in 1853, saw it as the romance of Yankee ingenuity (see pg. 28). Oregon City became an artistic icon fully as much as the Indian dancers, the forlorn totems, the deserted Indian huts, and the angry mountain. The theme of American progress had taken its place as part of the enduring mythology of the Pacific Northwest. Thus, already by the early 1850s, three primary mythic images had come to dominate the iconography of the Pacific Northwest: stunning, larger-than-life scenery, exotic Indian culture, and scenes of American progress that by implication forever pushed the Canadians north and beckoned a whole new people to fill up the remote region.

John Mix Stanley, an American painter born near Buffalo, New York, but working out of Detroit, was another who became mesmerized by the deeds and works of George Catlin. He had known Paul Kane in Detroit and they often must have discussed Catlin's gallery. Each artist set out in his separate way to duplicate and even surpass it. Stanley has, until the recent work of Julia Schimmel,[29] remained something of a mystery to art historians because it was assumed that the

---

[29] Julia Ann Schimmel, "John Mix Stanley and Imagery of the West in Nineteenth-Century Art," Ph.D. diss., New York University, 1983.

majority of his work had been destroyed in a fire at the Smithsonian Institution in 1865. However, Schimmel has been able to locate more than 200 of his surviving works—enough to make a judgment of his widely varied artistic achievements. Quite possibly Stanley's most interesting work was done in the Southwest when he painted the Comanches in Texas in 1843, and when he traveled west with General Stephen W. Kearny's army in the Mexican War. The lithographs that accompany Lieutenant William H. Emory's report on Kearny's march to California do not begin to do justice to the beautiful oil landscapes that Stanley painted while on that memorable military campaign in the Southwest in 1846-1847.

Stanley's best known works are those executed for the Isaac I. Stevens[30] reconnaissance for a northern Pacific railroad route in 1853-1854. In comparatively recent times original watercolors of the paintings done on this expedition have come to light. One can now compare them with the Sarony, Major, and Knapp lithographs that accompanied the official

[30] Isaac Ingalls Stevens (1818-1862), a West Point graduate and veteran of the Mexican War, campaigned for Franklin Pierce in the presidential election of 1852. In recognition of this support, Pierce in 1853 appointed Stevens governor of the newly created Washington Territory, and also made him chief of the northern Pacific railroad survey and territorial Indian agent. When Stevens headed west to take his post in Olympia, his party of surveyors, scientists, and soldiers investigated much of the northern Plains and Rockies, as well as the Columbia Plateau, for potential railroad routes. As governor, the highly capable and controversial Stevens played the dominant role in a turbulent period of Indian wars and political disputes, before he was elected territorial delegate to Congress in 1857. During the Civil War he achieved the rank of major general before he was killed, in 1862, at Chantilly, Virginia. He was shot down while charging, with banner in hand, toward Confederate positions on the same battlefield where his son, Hazard Stevens, was wounded.

U.S. Government "Pacific Railroad Survey Reports."[31] In the area of our interest, these scenes include views of the missions, Palouse Falls, Grand Coulee, Kettle Falls, Puget Sound, and Mount Rainier, as well as meetings in the deep woods with the Nez Perce Indians. Clearly, the originals of the landscapes are far more striking than the lithographs which were not true chromolithographs, but the genre scenes perhaps were aided or improved by the lithographers.[32] Stanley's paintings varied more widely in quality than perhaps any other American artist. Some field works in oil are strikingly beautiful. Others, in watercolor, are careless and often absurd in perspective and detail.

His finished studio works can be impressive, but also incredibly artificial. Some of his works show how well Stanley could paint when he had time to complete a picture properly. His views of the Columbia River and of Oregon City also demonstrate two main themes of Pacific Northwest iconography— those of the wonderful wilderness and Yankee progress. Curiously, in view of his Catlinesque mission, Stanley appears to have done little in the way of ethnographic painting, but

---

[31] In addition to the Stevens expedition between the 47th and 49th parallels, other major survey parties inspected potential railroad routes along the 38th, 35th, and 32nd parallels, and various minor reconnaissances also were completed. From 1855 to 1861, Congress authorized the release of an important multi-volume set of reports outlining these far-ranging investigations across the entire West. The most significant volume in regard to the Pacific Northwest was Isaac I. Stevens, *Narrative and Final Report of Explorations. . . .* (Pacific Railroad Surveys, Vol. 12), 36th Cong., 1st Sess., Senate Ex. Doc. 78, Washington, D. C., 1860. Eventually, four of the five original transcontinental railroads followed along general routes recommended by the Pacific railroad surveyors.

[32] Lithography involved making prints from a metal plate or flat stone by a method based on repulsion between grease and water. A design was applied to the flat surface with grease, and then water and ink were applied alternately. The greasy portions of the imprint absorbed the ink, whereas the wet parts repelled it. Chromolithography, on the other hand, required use of a series of plates, to each of which was applied a different colored ink to produce a multi-color illustration.

very probably his Indian portraits and ethnographic works, except for a few surviving ones at the Denver Public Library, are what fell to the flames in the Smithsonian fire, and what we are left with are his landscapes and view paintings. Because of this, his known Northwest work does not match that of Paul Kane.

U.S. Army private Gustavus Sohon, from Tilsit, Germany, is perhaps best remembered in the Northwest for his careful pencil portraits of many of the last great Northwest Indian chieftains. In 1855 he attended treaty councils that eventually ceded millions of acres of land in Washington and Oregon territories[33] to white settlers. His exact drawings of the individual chiefs on these occasions have excited the admiration of anthropologists and historians alike. Another Sohon, however, is also of great interest. That is the Sohon of the Stevens northern Pacific railroad expedition and the Mullan wagon road project.[34] Here he seemed preoccupied with the difficulties of crossing the Hellgate River, near present-day Missoula, Montana. He drew this scene in winter and summer in several versions. Most are charming sketches of men in dire straits. At least one is so dramatically rendered it bears direct comparison with Theodore Gericault's famous *The Raft of the*

[33] Washington Territory at that time included all of present-day Washington, the northern panhandle of Idaho, and that portion of Montana located west of the Continental Divide. Sohon was assigned to Governor Stevens's party and attended the Walla Walla, Flathead, Blackfoot, and Spokane councils.

[34] From 1857 to 1862, Lieutenant John Mullan (1830-1909) directed the construction of the 624-mile-long "Mullan Road," extending eastward from Fort Walla Walla, across the Bitterroots and Rockies, to Fort Benton on the Montana plains. This famous, but rugged, trail provided a key transportation link between the uppermost points of steamboat navigation on the Missouri and Columbia river systems.

Medusa (1819).[35] It is perhaps Sohon's most fully developed drawing—but not his best work. An insight into Sohon's extraordinary skill as an artist can be seen in the wonderfully delicate watercolor panels that form the originals for Stanley's panorama of "The Main Chain of the Rocky Mountains Seen From the East" in the "Pacific Railroad Survey Reports." Clearly, Private Sohon, a self-taught artist, had incredible talent that he never really developed as he confined himself to penciled Indian portraits and modest sketches such as one of the "Great Falls of the Spokane River."

The federal government in the 1850s provided the most significant opportunities for artists to sketch or paint the Pacific Northwest. Best known of these opportunities is, of course, the Pacific railroad surveys. But the most striking art derived from the artists working on the U.S. Coast and Geodetic Survey (prior to 1871 called the U.S. Coast Survey). This federal employment of artists in the Northwest is important. In the conventional view of the history of American art we are continually told, following the generalizations of the French traveler, Count Alexis de Tocqueville,[36] that the United States offered little aid and comfort to artists—or for that matter, scientists. By implication, America had no soul and no mind—only a nose for commerce. Neill Harris in the widely

---

[35] French painter Jean Louis Andre Theodore Gericault (1791-1824) first exhibited his enormous canvas *The Raft of the Medusa* at the Louvre in 1819. With Romantic/ Realist pathos, it depicts an infamous incident where shipwrecked passengers were cast adrift on a raft for many days. Few of the unfortunate souls survived. Blame for the tragedy was directed at the French authorities, who in turn attempted to suppress Gericault's spectacular depiction of the event. With this publicity, it became one of the most popular and influential paintings of all time. The *Medusa* was next shown in England, where for two years Gericault charged viewing fees and acquired a large amount of money. Ironically, this highly influential artist only exhibited three works during his short lifetime. He died in Paris in 1824.

[36] The French nobleman, Alexis de Tocqueville (1805-1859), traveled throughout much of the East and the transappalachian West in 1831-1832, and later published a well-known critique of American society and culture, *Democracy in America,* 1st American edition, 1835.

read, *The Artist in American Society: The Formative Years, 1790-1860* (1966), makes this point in exhaustive detail. But a preliminary study of federal expenditures for art and science in four major federal agencies before the Civil War—the Army, the Navy, the Coast Survey, and the Patent Office—indicates that perhaps as much as one-third of the annual budget went into expenditures on work in science and art. The federal government employed literally thousands of people engaged in these enterprises in the period before the Civil War in expeditions along our coasts, across the continent from east to west, and north to south along the great inland rivers, and on at least fifteen major extra-continental exploring expeditions ranging around the globe. At no time until the present day, including the New Deal Era, has such a portion of the federal budget been allocated to science and to art.

Even if this point is conceded, however, the rejoinder often is that the science was really technology and the art was strictly utilitarian. The work of the U.S. Coast and Geodetic Survey on the Northwest Coast provides an interesting test. In its scientific work, geodesy and astronomy, the U.S. Coast Survey set a standard for the world by 1870. The capstone of its achievements came with the great triangulated arc across the North American continent, which made the exact measurement of the globe possible. As for art, let us turn to the work of two astonishing painters, James Madison Alden and Cleveland Rockwell.

These artists' primary duties were to draw maps of the coast indicating shoals, harbors, shorelines, and depths. But since, before radar, most sea captains approached land by visual sighting, artists like James Madison Alden and Cleveland Rockwell, and even James Abbott McNeill Whistler, who engraved "Whistler's Mother" while working in a rock formation in the Santa Barbara Channel on the Coast Survey, were required to paint the shorelines in such a way as to provide visual guides to approaching vessels. This is a form of topographic art that goes back to the early Renaissance. It is an art that, however, spawned a new genre, "view painting," which later gained respectability as landscape painting. Alden and Rockwell serve admirably to track this sequence of artistic evolution. They became outstanding view painters, panoramists, and landscape (or seascape) painters.

James Madison Alden, who had studied art with Thomas Weir Cummings in New York, a founder of the National Academy of Design, first served aboard the USS *Active*, a Coast Survey vessel charting the Pacific coastline in the 1850s. But as part of his duties, Alden also went up the Columbia River. In addition, he became the principal artist on the Northwest Boundary Survey between the United States and Canada in 1859-1860. Thus, he trekked all over the Pacific Northwest as far inland as the Continental Divide. The water-colors he produced were varied and spectacular—far beyond mere utilitarian drawings and even view paintings. They were stunning landscapes of giant canyons, rivers, and vast panoramic views of the Strait of Juan de Fuca and Puget Sound. Clearly, Alden saw himself as an artist.

The same applies even more to Cleveland Rockwell. Rockwell's major work on the Coast Survey came between 1868 and 1891. He had started his work on the Pacific Coast in 1857, but was forced to take time out to serve as chief topographer to General William Tecumseh Sherman during the Civil War. It seems clear that Rockwell had been an artist from the beginning. Like Alden, he studied under Cummings in

New York. But he also appears to have studied the works of Frederick Church, Martin Johnson Heade, Sanford Robinson Gifford, John F. Kensett, Alfred Jacob Miller, Fitzhugh Lane, William Sydney Mount, Thomas Birch, William Bradford, and Winslow Homer.[37] With these influences, Rockwell became perhaps the West Coast's only clearly identifiable (though neglected) luminist marine painter. In the stillness and diffused light of his paintings, one clearly sees echoes of Lane and Kensett. In some, the golden glow of Gifford permeates the scene. In addition, any number of influences by the other painters mentioned above are apparent. Certainly, in any serious survey of American luminism, Cleveland Rockwell must be included.

That he was well aware of himself as an artist is also clear. For decades he was a central figure in the San Francisco art scene where his pictures were often exhibited in public and private galleries and shows, and were frequently sold. Even the canny Scotsman, John Muir, owned a "Columbia River" by Rockwell. In addition, in the spirit of Frederick Church and Albert Bierstadt, his contemporaries, Rockwell sailed to the cold reaches of Alaska to paint, and journeyed to the Magdalena River of South America in the footsteps of Humboldt and La Condamine. He was no mere Coast Survey draftsman, and his career as an artist deserves more study than it has received thus far, despite the splendid pioneering work of Dr. and Mrs. Franz Stenzel of Portland, Oregon.[38]

But what of the relationship of Alden's and Rockwell's work to Pacific Northwest iconography? Simply answered,

[37] Rockwell seems to have been principally influenced by the works of the luminists, Heade, Kensett, Gifford and Lane. See John Wilmerding, et al., *American Light, the Luminist Movement, 1850-1875* (Washington, D.C.: The National Gallery of Art, 1980).

[38] Franz Stenzel, *Cleveland Rockwell, Scientist and Artist, 1837-1907* (Portland: Oregon Historical Society, 1972).

they were the painters of scenic grandeur. They were to the
Pacific Northwest what Bierstadt and Moran were to the
Rocky Mountains, the Sierras, and Yellowstone. Alden, the
cruder, less schooled of the two, dealt in dramatic sweeping
images of natural wonders and huge panoramas. Rockwell
specialized in "still and solitary grandeur." Both were painters
of the sublime—Pacific Northwest version. Both focused on
nature, relatively unspoiled, the way John Muir and John
Ruskin would have it. Both eschewed images of bustling progress in favor of either vast, empty, towering grandeur, or quiet
pre-industrial marine scenes dominated by fascinating varieties
of almost holy light. They were perhaps the last eyewitness
painters to portray the Pacific Northwest before boosterism
and images of progress and energy came to dominate the
scene.

By the turn of the century railroads were the rage.
Railroads like the Northern Pacific, the Great Northern, and
the Oregon Railway and Navigation Company brought farm-
ing, industry, and tourists to a Pacific Northwest that began to
suffer from a schizophrenic divided image of itself. Railroad
picture publications, *Wonderland Magazine* and *The Truth
about the Palouse Country*, had it both ways. Industry was
really a machine functioning efficiently and energetically in the
grandeur of nature—part mountainous wilderness, part
flourishing garden. The railroad made the Gem Mine feasible
in wilderness Idaho. It fostered sawmills on Puget Sound. It
helped to harness the truly "wondrous" power of Spokane
Falls; and it probably caused calamities like the great fire at

Wallace, Idaho, July 27, 1890. Everything was up-to-date by now in the Pacific Northwest—at least iconographically.

But the railroads were not the climax. This came with the automobile. Railroads were not flexible enough. Autos could ramble almost anywhere, sampling industrial citified delights or nature's wonders. Something of the spirit of the new automobile age, the sense of modern progress, the wonders of technology, and the eternal sense of scenic grandeur were all captured in significant ways by a new kind of artist who, until now, has been almost unknown. This is the engineer/photographer, Samuel Christopher Lancaster. Lancaster was the civil engineer who designed and built the great highway along the Columbia River, as he put it, "through the Cascade Mountains to the Sea." Constructed before World War I, it was an engineering marvel—the conqueror of a vast, rugged, yet incomparably scenic terrain. It was, for the Pacific Northwest, a new Oregon Trail.

Lancaster was justly proud of it as an engineering feat. But as an artist, he went even further. As early as 1914, within four or five years of the earliest experiments in color photography, he invented a color reproduction process that would match his engineering feats. With his spectacular color photographs, he took us over the great Columbia Highway from the Cascades, to Multnomah Falls, to Portland in the evening, looking like nothing so much as a James Abbott McNeill Whistler painting. He even gave us a prophetic view of the burned-over district that now rests dominated by Mt. St. Helens, then as now a disturbed element in the complex land that is the Pacific Northwest—a land that includes Portland at twilight, Albert Bierstadt's picturesque Multnomah Falls, and the endless utilitarian geometry of the great Columbia Plain today. ■

ARTISTS VIEW THE LAND OF PROMISE:

A NINETEENTH-CENTURY PORTFOLIO

Drayton worked as an engraver in Philadelphia from around 1819 until 1838 when he joined the United States Exploring Expedition under Charles Wilkes. He and Alfred Agate sketched the American northwest coast as well as the coast of Antarctica and over 200 Pacific islands. Drayton Harbor and Drayton Passage, west of Anderson Island in Puget Sound, were named for him.

Indians Playing the Spear Game, "Foothills of Mt. Hood" by Joseph Drayton
Oregon Historical Society, Portland, Oregon

Fur Traders—Walla Walla by Joseph Drayton
Oregon Historical Society, Portland, Oregon

Fort Walla Walla was a North West Company fort established in 1818 at the junction of the Walla Walla and Colum-bia rivers. McLean was the Factor and most likely is the man in the tailcoat.

  Drayton probably did not visit Fort Walla Walla. The sketch shows tree-covered hills in the background and there are no forests in the semiarid region in which the historic fort was located. Drayton can only be credited with reworking someone else's drawing.

Chimikane Mission Station by Joseph Drayton
Oregon Historical Society, Portland, Oregon

*Since Drayton never was near the mission, this scene probably was sketched from an original drawing by a member
of Lt. Robert Johnson's exploring party. While in the mission vicinity between June 14 and 21, Johnson was
accompanied by T. Waldron, a marine sergeant; a servant; and Pickering and Brackenridge, botanists with the
expedition.*

   R. E. Johnson (a member of the Wilkes Expedition) to Mary Richardson Walker:

      *I have traveled many a weary mile, o'er the wild wastes of Oregon, where chance turned my steps to the
      hospitable door of the mission on the Spokane. There my thoughts were turned to home by the domestic
      comforts I witnessed and I left with a grateful heart for the cordial welcome I received.—June 15, 1841*

Mary Richardson Walker autograph album, Washington State University Libraries, Pullman, Washington.

CHARLES ANDREW GEYER, 1809-1853

In 1843 and 1844, Geyer, a German botanist, traveled with Sir William Drummond Stewart to the Wind River Mountains, then proceeded with a caravan of Catholic missionaries to Flathead Mission. He continued traveling throughout the Oregon Country noting and collecting botanical specimens. Geyer explored the Spokane country with the help of Cushing Eells and Elkanah Walker, missionaries of the American Board who were stationed at Tshimakain Mission. On the 13th of November, 1844, Geyer left Fort Vancouver to sail for London. He eventually returned to Dresden and practiced commercial gardening at Meissen, and became editor of *Chronik des Gartenwesens,* an independent garden journal.

Geyer's botanical work in the western United States was of such importance that no less than thirteen plants have been named in his honor.

Tshimakain by Charles Andrew Geyer
Washington State University Libraries, Pullman, Washington

I arrived (at Tshimakain) in the midst of winter 1843, almost exhausted by want of food, having been lost and wandering alone in the mountains and woods for thirteen days where the snow was 2 and 3 feet deep. To a brother missionary of the same body I owe the means of visiting another new field, the Highlands of the Nez-Perces Indians [Spalding Mission on the Clearwater River] where he accompanied me on my excursions, and also afforded facilities to investigate the flowery Koos Kooskee valley over again, where previous botanists have but cursorily passed.—Charles A. Geyer

W. J. Hooker. *London Journal of Botany,* volumes 4-5, 1845-46.

Father Point assisted Pierre De Smet in the founding of Catholic Missions in the Northwest. Although he had no formal art training, Father Point carefully recorded his experiences and observations of the West in what some critics consider a primitive way. His religious paintings are filled with symbols of his faith in the pietistic tradition of his native France, however, drawings of the Indians and their customs are free from these symbols and are revealing portrayals of a rapidly changing way of life among the Indians in the 1840s.

Three Indian Portraits by Father Nicholas Point
Washington State University Libraries, Pullman, Washington

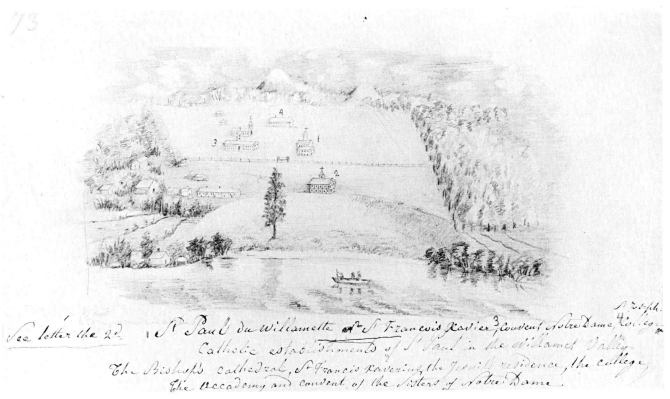

St. Paul's Mission on the Willamette by Father Nicholas Point
Washington State University Libraries, Pullman, Washington

While he was in Europe, Kane met George Catlin whose paintings of Indian culture had become the talk of London. Back in Canada, Kane began a long-time commitment to sketching and recording the Indian way of life. Gaining the support of Sir George Simpson of the Hudson's Bay Company, Kane traveled westward across the continent, reaching the Oregon Country in 1846. He produced over one hundred oils from his pencil sketches and watercolors, and his reputation as a pioneer Canadian artist was established.

Self-portrait by Paul Kane
Stark Museum of Art, Orange, Texas

Kettle Falls, Fort Colvile by Paul Kane
Stark Museum of Art, Orange, Texas

French-Canadian employees called these falls Les Chaudieres. *Yankee traders and settlers simply translated the name into English.*

The Man That Always Rides by Paul Kane
Royal Ontario Museum, Toronto, Canada

Graves at I-Eh-Nus by Paul Kane
Stark Museum of Art, Orange, Texas

Interior of a Clallam Winter Lodge by Paul Kane
National Gallery of Canada, Ottawa, Canada

Medicine Mask Dance by Paul Kane
Royal Ontario Museum, Toronto, Canada

Flathead and Child by Paul Kane
The Montreal Museum of Fine Arts, Montreal, Canada

Cow-Wacham, *a member of the Cowlitz Indian tribe, lived on the shores of the Cowlitz River near its confluence with the Columbia. The original sketch was made in 1846 and printed in London as a lithograph in 1859.*

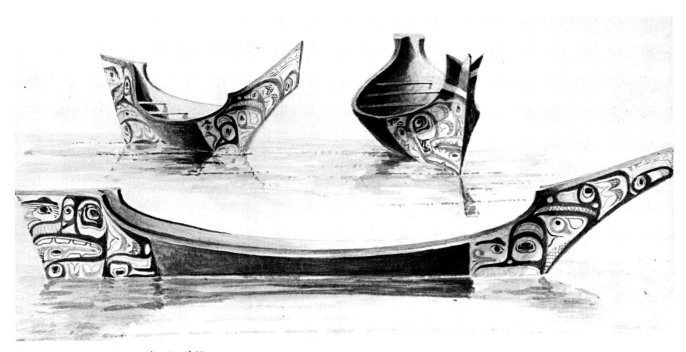

Northwest Coast Canoes by Paul Kane
Royal Ontario Museum, Toronto, Canada

Medicine Masks of the Northwest Coast Tribes by Paul Kane
Stark Museum of Art, Orange, Texas

Catching Salmon on the Columbia River by Paul Kane
Stark Museum of Art, Orange, Texas

The Cascades by Paul Kane
Stark Museum of Art, Orange, Texas

The Cascades on the Columbia River no longer exist, having been inundated by Bonneville Dam. In 1805, Lewis and Clark applied the name "Great Shute" to the upper rapids. In 1825, John Work of the Hudson's Bay Company was the first to apply the name Cascades.

Oregon City Seen from the Opposite Shore beside Waterfall by Paul Kane
Royal Ontario Museum, Toronto, Canada

The church in the center of the picture was built in 1842 and opened for services in 1844. It was one of the first buildings erected exclusively for religious purposes in the Oregon Country. Dr. John McLoughlin platted the Oregon City town site. The Molallas ceded their lands around the Oregon City site in 1850 for $22,000.

Mt. St. Helens with Smoke Cone by Paul Kane
Stark Museum of Art, Orange, Texas

Mt. St. Helens Erupting by Paul Kane
Stark Museum of Art, Orange, Texas

George Vancouver named Mt. St. Helens in honor of the British ambassador to Spain at that time. The Indian name for the peak was Low-We-Not-Thlat.

Not all nineteenth-century artists who tried to draw or paint the Pacific Northwest were of the caliber of Sohon, Kane, or Stanley. The following sketch of the eruption of Mt. St. Helens was drawn by Stevens, a young man from Milwaukie, Oregon, in 1853.

Mt. St. Helens in Eruption from a letter written by Charles Stevens, 1853
Oregon Historical Society, Portland, Oregon

Stevens's sketch of St. Helens was drawn on the back of a letter he wrote to "Lydia" on April 10, 1853. In this letter, he passes on several pieces of misinformation to his friend:

Lydia,

On the opposite side of this I have drawed [sic] a little sketch of Mount St. Hellen [sic], as it appears way down on the mouth of the Columbia River, it is not correct, but it will let you see how these mountains look. Where I saw the sketch, is about two hundred miles from the mountains, and I suppose it might be seen one hundred miles out at sea.

The little black spot near the top is a hole, where the fire and smoke comes out. It runs way up above the clouds as you will see the spots near the bottom looks like black lava. Mount Hoods [sic] shape is nearly the shape of this. The river in the picture is the Columbia.

The river comes in from the right though it looks as though it did not go any further. The whole of this mountain is covered with the whitest snow way down below where you can see it. They are the grandest, the most beautiful sights it appears to me, that a person can look upon. They are so high no one can go half way to the top.

HENRY JAMES WARRE, 1819-1898

British army officer Henry Warre was sent on a military survey for the British government to the Oregon Country in 1845-46. During the trip, Warre and his companion, Lieutenant Mervin Vavasour, pretended to be gentlemen of leisure while obtaining information on the area in case military operations were necessary against the United States. Although Warre and Vavasour's final report did not affect the outcome of the border dispute between Great Britain and the United States, the sketches and writing done by Warre are of historical importance. His journal is an interesting record of a period of rapid change on the Northwest frontier. Warre's watercolor drawings were reproduced and published in *Sketches in North America and the Oregon Territory* in London in 1848.

Fort Colvile by Henry James Warre
American Antiquarian Society, Worcester, Massachusetts

George Simpson selected the site for Fort Colvile on his first trip through the Pacific Northwest, and workers began construction in the autumn and spring of 1825-26. Andrew Colvile, the person after whom the fort was named, served as a director, and later a governor, of the Hudson's Bay Company. The following is George Simpson's description of the locality:

> *Thursday, April 14th [1825]. . . We selected a beautiful point on the South side about 3/4ths of a Mile above the Portage where there is abundance of fine Timber and the situation elegible [sic] in every point of view. An excellent Farm can be made at this place where as much Grain and potatoes may be raised as would feed all the Natives of the Columbia and a sufficient number of Cattle and Hogs to supply his Majestys [sic] Navy with Beef and Pork. . . . Lined out the Site of the Establisht 150 feet Square on a bank facing and commanding a view of the River and I have taken the liberty of naming it Fort Colvile.*

Fur Trade and Empire, George Simpson's *Journal,* 1824-25, edited by Frederick Merk, Howard University Press, 1931.

Puget's Sound by Henry James Warre
American Antiquarian Society, Worcester, Massachusetts

Address about the Northwest presented to the American Geographical and Statistics Society, December 2, 1858, by Isaac I. Stevens:

> *If you look to the Rocky Mountain region, between the 46th and 49th parallels, you will find that it is essentially a country of prairies. West of the Bitter Root chain of mountains, a great plain stretches to the Cascade mountains, on the west, and from the 48th to below the 46th parallel. This prairie region is, for the most part, well watered, well grassed, and furnishes a large portion of arable land. . . . Puget's sound is admitted by all naval and military gentlemen who ever visited its waters, to be the most remarkable roadstead on the shores of any ocean. . . . It can be entered by any wind, is scarcely ever obstructed by fog, and is the nearest point to the great ports of Asia of any harbor on our western coast.*

Falls of the Peloos River by Henry James Warre
Holograph drawing from the American Antiquarian Society, Worcester, Massachusetts

From Warre's Journal, *volume 2, pp. 1556-57, 1587-90:*

> *We were riding apparently over a vast undulating prairie, from whence the view was magnificent extending far into the distance and bounded by the Blue Mountains which were covered to the base, with Snow. This apparently rolling Prairie is intersected by vast gullies of greater or less breadth and through one of these the Peloos River has its almost subterranean course.—We heard the heavy roar of a Cataract, and spurring our Horses, for about half a mile from the course we were following; we came upon the brink of an immense circular chasm of a great depth and breadth, into which the whole body of the River was falling in perpendicular height about 200 feet—the grandeur of the scene is indescribable, but very beautiful—the numerous rainbows and curious pointed basaltic Rocks the spray and the noise and the wildness of the boundless, barren prairie above are such as can hardly be conveyed in the rapid and imperfect sketch I made at the time. . .*

Palouse Falls by Henry James Warre
Washington State University Libraries, Pullman, Washington

This lithograph was made from Warre's original sketch shown on page 62. The lithographer has added two Indian figures in the foreground.

Although George Catlin is known primarily for his ethnography of tribes living along the Missouri and Platte rivers, he also painted and drew the Indians of the Pacific Northwest. Much of this Pacific Northwest art can be found in *Life Among the Indians* and *Last Rambles*, published after a voyage up the Pacific Coast in the 1850s.

Growing up on the frontier, Catlin became fascinated with Indian culture at an early age. Although he took up the study of law in 1818, he soon abandoned the profession and taught himself to paint. By 1823, he came under the influence of Philadelphia artists Thomas Sully, John Neagle, and especially Rembrandt Peale. From 1829 to the end of 1838 Catlin produced more than 600 sketches and paintings of Indian life and culture. During the 1850s Catlin traveled extensively in South America and along the western coast of North America. In 1871, the year before he died, a large collection of Catlin's South and North American Indian drawings was displayed at the Smithsonian Institution.

Excavating a Canoe, by Nayas Indians, British Columbia by George Catlin
National Gallery of Art, Paul Mellon Collection, Washington, D. C.

A Whale Ashore, on the western coast of Vancouver, and being harpooned and dissected by the Klahoquat Indians, 1855 by George Catlin
National Gallery of Art, Paul Mellon Collection, Washington, D. C.

Flathead Indians Fishing by George Catlin
National Gallery of Art, Paul Mellon Collection, Washington, D. C.

Catlin's ability as an ethnographic artist is apparent in this 1861 drawing of a small group of Pacific Coast Indians. In the foreground, he has sketched a blanket-draped chief overseeing a salmon catch. In the center of the illustration, he positioned the chief's wife loading fish into a basket; on her back, she carries a small child undergoing the head-flattening process. The artist completed the drawing by including two boys with bows and harpoon-tipped arrows in the background.

JOHN MIX STANLEY, 1814-1872

Born in New York, Stanley moved to Detroit in 1834 where he worked as a house and sign painter. There he met James Bowman, an artist, who gave him his first lessons in portrait painting. Stanley visited Washington, D.C. and seems to have been associated briefly with a daguerreotypist who was experimenting with photography.

In 1846 Stanley journeyed to Santa Fe and joined Colonel Stephen Watts Kearney's military expedition to California as a member of its scientific staff. He remained in the West traveling to San Francisco and Oregon in 1847-48, and returned to the East Coast via the Hawaiian Islands in 1849.

Stanley was appointed to accompany Isaac Stevens's survey of a northern transcontinental railroad route to the Pacific Coast in 1853. After returning to the East, he prepared his drawings for illustrating Stevens's railroad reports.

The Dalles by John Mix Stanley
Pacific Railroad Reports, volume 12, 1855-61

At the Dalles, the river [Columbia] is compressed into a narrow channel, 300 feet wide and half a mile long, between high basaltic rocks, flat on the top: the river descends fifty feet in two miles. The Dalles is situated in an amphitheater, extending several miles to the north-west, which is enclosed by basaltic walls.

Charles Wilkes, *Western America Including California and Oregon With Maps of Those Regions, and of "The Sacramento Valley,"* Philadelphia: Lea and Blanchard, 1849.

Kettle Falls, Columbia River by John Mix Stanley
Pacific Railroad Reports, volume 12, 1855-61.

At one time this was one of the greatest Indian fisheries of the Northwest.

Grand Coulee by John Mix Stanley
Pacific Railroad Reports, volume 12, 1855-61

Chemakane Mission by John Mix Stanley
Pacific Railroad Reports, volume 12, 1855-61

Sohon emigrated to America in 1842 and enlisted in the United States Army in 1852. He served under Governor Isaac Stevens on the exploration of a northern railroad route from the Mississippi River to Puget Sound in 1853. Sohon then accompanied Lieutenant Rufus Saxton to the interior on a commissary trip. Stevens assigned Sohon to Lieutenant John Mullan, who was to stay in the interior and make climatological and topographical observations during the winter of 1853-54. With his linguistic talents, Sohon provided valuable assistance to Mullan because he was able to gain knowledge of the mountain passes and river systems from the Indians.

Governor Stevens transferred Sohon to his command in 1855 and used him as an interpreter and liaison with the Indians during treaty negotiations. After this work was completed, Sohon served with Colonel George Wright's command in the 1858 campaign against the Spokane, Coeur d'Alene, and other northern Plateau tribes. Three of Sohon's sketches from this period appear on pages 72, 73, and 74. By 1860, he joined Lieutenant Mullan's party of road builders in constructing the Mullan Road across the northern Rockies between Fort Walla Walla and Fort Benton.

Crossing the Hellgate, 1854 by Gustavus Sohon
Pacific Railroad Reports, volume 12, 1855-61

Great Falls of the Spokane River, W. T. by Gustavus Sohon
Holograph drawing from Washington State University Libraries, Pullman, Washington

Camp on the Spokane River—Sept. 6, 1858 by Gustavus Sohon
Holograph drawing from Washington State University Libraries, Pullman, Washington

View of Snake River at Mouth of Tukanon Showing Fort Taylor and Bluffs by Gustavus Sohon
Holograph drawing from Washington State University Libraries, Pullman, Washington

JAMES MADISON ALDEN, 1834-1922

Alden was a topographer for the United States Coast Survey from 1854 to 1857. From 1857 through 1860 he was official artist for the United States-Canada boundary survey. The Civil War interrupted the final phases of the survey and only a few watercolor sketches from this period of Alden's career were saved. Because of the war, the federal government never published the results of the west coast or northwestern boundary surveys.

According to Franz Stenzel in his book *James Madison Alden*, he was "a mild-mannered man . . . thus his views of nature were peaceful and serene." None of Alden's drawings or watercolors show any turmoil in nature; no storms, no wind-tossed waves, or a clashing of elements.

Nanaimo Indian Village by James Madison Alden
Provincial Archives of British Columbia, Victoria, British Columbia

Alden painted this Indian village on Vancouver Island, British Columbia, in 1858.

Astoria by James Madison Alden
Washington State Historical Society, Tacoma, Washington

Alden sketched Astoria while on board the Active *in 1854.*

Astoria at the mouth of the Columbia was the first permanent settlement in the Oregon Country. Duncan McDougal, a partner of Astor's in the Pacific Fur Company, chose the site for the post in 1811.

Fort Vancouver by James Madison Alden
Beinecke Library, Yale University, New Haven, Connecticut

Alden painted the raising of the colors at Fort Vancouver in the recently formed Washington Territory in 1854. The fort was originally built by the Hudson's Bay Company in the mid-1820's on the right bank of the Columbia River. George Simpson, deputy governor of the Hudson's Bay Company, stated, "The object of naming it (Fort Vancouver) after that distinguished navigator is to identify our claim to the soil and trade with his discovery of the river and coast on behalf of Great Britain. If the honorable committee do not approve the name, it can be changed." After the settlement of the boundary dispute between Great Britain and the United States, it became a U.S. military post in 1849.

Fort Nisqually by James Madison Alden
Washington State Historical Society, Tacoma, Washington

Fort Nisqually was sketched by Alden in July, 1857. Two forts by this name were built by the Hudson's Bay Company on different sites in the vicinity of the present town of Steilacoom. The first, built in 1833, was on Nisqually Reach near the water's edge. A decade later the establishment was relocated and called Nisqually House. It later was operated by the Puget Sound Agricultural Company, a subsidiary of the Hudson's Bay Company.

The Fourth of July was celebrated for the first time in the [Oregon] territory in 1841 by the crew of Wilkes'[s] ships at Puget Sound. . . . The Fourth fell on Sunday, so the festivities, consisting of a barbecue, games, Indian horse-racing and the firing of salutes, were held on the day following. Sailors and marines marched to the British fur-trading establishment at Nisqually, gave three rousing cheers, and waited for an acknowledgment from the fort. The return hurrahs were but feebly given by a few voices which lacked enthusiasm, a circumstance which Wilkes records was the cause of much merriment among the seamen.

Charles Henry Carey, *History of Oregon*, Chicago-Portland: Pioneer Historical Publishing Co., 1922, p. 425.

*Straits of Rosario, Cypress Island, and Strawberry Harbor on the Right— Hautboy Island in the Centre—Mt.
Constitution and Orcas Island in the Distance* by James Madison Alden
Record Group 76, National Archives, Washington, D.C.

*Alden executed this work in 1858, at the beginning of the Northwestern Boundary Survey. The British were claiming
the middle, or Rosario Strait, as the channel marking the boundary delineating their claims, while the United States
argued that the proper boundary lay in the the Strait of Haro. In 1841 Commander Wilkes had named the strait
Ringgold Channel in honor of Cadwalader Ringgold, one of the expedition's officers. It was renamed Rosario Strait in
1847 by Captain Kelley to honor the patroness of a Spanish ship, the* San Carlos.

Puget Sound Agricultural Company Station, San Juan Island by James Madison Alden
Washington State Historical Society, Tacoma, Washington

Sketched by Alden in 1857, the Puget Sound Agricultural Company was organized by the Hudson's Bay Company in 1839. As fur trading became less profitable, the Hudson's Bay Company turned to growing grain and breeding livestock in the Pacific Northwest.

H. B. Co. Fort Langley, Left Bank of Fraser River by James Madison Alden
Record Group 76, National Archives, Washington, D.C.

Alden painted this watercolor in 1858 on a northwestern boundary survey trip. An Indian village is visible across the Fraser River.

Kootenay River, Junction With Elk River, View from Trail on Right Bank by James Madison Alden
Record Group 76, National Archives, Washington, D.C.

The Kootenay River begins in British Columbia on the western slopes of the Rocky Mountains and crosses the 49th parallel twice before entering the Columbia River.

View from Monument at Summit Looking W. along 49th Parallel, Highest Peak Kintla Range Bears S. 25 W.
by James Madison Alden
Record Group 76, National Archives, Washington, D.C.

The 1860 season was devoted to surveying the international boundary from the coast to the crest of the Rockies. Alden followed the Fraser River, which flowed close to the 49th parallel for nearly 75 miles before turning north. He then gained access to the 49th parallel by using rivers running north or south from the border; the Columbia, Kootenay, Similkameen, Kettle, and Granby. In October, 1860, twenty-six-year-old James Alden stood on the summit of the Rocky Mountains, his mission accomplished. He painted two views from this apex, the above watercolor looking west in the direction from which he had come, and another looking east across Chief Mountain Lake.

Downing made numerous landscape sketches while he was surveying trails and river systems in the territories of Washington, Idaho, Montana, and the Dakotas during the late 1800s. A sketchbook at the Washington State Historical Society contains some 144 sketches and watercolors completed during four expeditions.

View of Lakes in Grande Coule by Alfred Downing
Washington State Historical Society, Tacoma, Washington

Old Fort Colvile Looking S.W. by Alfred Downing
Washington State Historical Society, Tacoma, Washington

Fort Colvile was located on the east bank of the Columbia River one mile above Kettle Falls. It was established in 1825 by the Hudson's Bay Company as a trading post, farm, defensive station, and supply depot for other company posts, and was completed during 1826 when company property and equipment were moved from old Spokane House. The fort site was flooded by the Franklin D. Roosevelt reservoir after Grand Coulee Dam was completed in 1939.

FORT COLVILLE, WASHINGTON TERRITORY.
RECENTLY ABANDONED BY THE WAR DEPARTMENT AS A MILITARY POST AFTER AN OCCUPANCY OF TWENTY-THREE YEARS.

U.S. Army Fort Colville in 1859 by Alfred Downing
Washington State Historical Society, Tacoma, Washington

This lithograph is of the American military post located approximately twenty miles southeast of the earlier Hudson's Bay Company's Fort Colvile. Constructed under orders from Major Pinkney Lugenbeel by companies A and E of the Ninth U. S. Infantry, it was intended to protect white settlers in the area from Indian attack. The post quickly became known as Fort Colville. Perhaps in error, or possibly for political reasons, Americans for many years had referred to the surrounding area as "the Colville Country," ignoring the proper British spelling of "Colvile." The U. S. Army adopted the Americanized spelling.

Camp in Moses Coule—July 21, 1880 by Alfred Downing
Washington State Historical Society, Tacoma, Washington

This large coulee formed by glacial action was named for Chief Moses, a Columbia Plains Indian diplomat and warrior.

A Glimpse of the Grande Coule by Alfred Downing
Washington State Historical Society, Tacoma, Washington

Grand Coulee was an old bed of the Columbia River during the Pleistocene. It was named by Lieutenant Charles Wilkes after a detachment of his men investigated the great chasm in 1841.

CLEVELAND ROCKWELL, 1836-1907

Educated in New York as an engineer, Rockwell joined the United States Coast Survey in 1856. During the Civil War, he was a topographer for the War Department; his maps were considered among the finest examples of mid-nineteenth century military cartography. Rockwell came to Oregon in 1868 as chief of the United States Coast Survey in the Northwest. His surveys of the Oregon coast, the Columbia River, and the Willamette River did much to encourage the development of navigation in the area.

Rockwell studied watercolor painting in England and on the continent and painted as a hobby all his life.

Salmon Fishing Grounds by Cleveland Rockwell
Oregon Historical Society, Portland, Oregon

The oil shows fishing boats at dawn at the mouth of the Columbia River around the year 1883.

Mt. Hood from Near Mouth of Willamette by Cleveland Rockwell
Oregon Historical Society, Portland, Oregon

ALFRED BURR, 18—-1942

Alfred Burr was employed for many years as an artist for the *West Shore* magazine. This lithograph taken from the *West Shore*, volume 10, June 1884, was typical of his work. Burr also worked for seventeen years with the Portland *Oregonian*. He died in Portland in 1942.

Three Scenes from Mt. Baker, Mt. Rainier, and Olympic Range by Alfred B. Burr
Oregon Historical Society, Portland, Oregon

CHARLES CLYDE BENTON COOKE, 1860-1933

Born in Salem, Oregon, Cooke studied in Germany at the Royal Academy and attended Willamette University. He was both a commercial artist and an instructor. His painting of the Upper Cascades was completed in 1879.

Upper Cascades Showing Cascade Block House by Charles Clyde Benton Cooke
Oregon Historical Society, Portland, Oregon

Photography used as a means of capturing and enhancing landscape images was introduced to the Pacific Northwest in the last half of the nineteenth century. Photographers routinely accompanied cartographic expeditions, such as Thomas Symons's surveys of the Columbia River in 1881 and 1891. In addition to aesthetic works by Carlton E. Watkins and Edward S. Curtis, images by Asahel Curtis, Barnard Stockbridge, and many less well-known commercial photographers were produced in large quantities throughout the latter nineteenth and early twentieth centuries.

Shepperd's Dell Bridge by Samuel Lancaster
Oregon Historical Society, Portland, Oregon

Samuel Lancaster was the engineer who designed the Columbia River Highway. This photograph, taken in 1915, shows a bridge on the newly completed road.

Multnomah Falls, photographer unknown
Oregon Historical Society, Portland, Oregon

This dream-like photograph of the famous falls east of Portland was commissioned by the Oregon Railway & Navigation Company.

Mitchell Point on the Columbia River Highway in 1915 by Weister Company
Oregon Historical Society, Portland, Oregon

Mt. St. Helens, circa 1905 from the Ashford Collection
Oregon Historical Society, Portland, Oregon

Portland, Oregon by J. J. Straub
Oregon Historical Society, Portland, Oregon

This photograph shows the city as it appeared about 1890. The dramatic snowcap on Mt. Hood in the background is a drawn-in "improvement" of reality.

In the 1870s, a new breed of artists appeared in the Pacific Northwest putting their talents in the service of promoting settlement and development in the region. No longer content to draw and sketch, they relied increasingly on the camera and new methods of printing; their work reflected the "boomer" mentality that dominated the American West in the late nineteenth and early twentieth centuries.

Railroads, towns, and land companies published countless pamphlets, brochures, and tracts extolling the virtues of various locales throughout the Pacific Northwest. These materials presented positive visual and written images designed to attract settlers and workers to the region. Typical of the genre are: *The Truth About the Palouse Country; The Land that Lures: Summer in the Pacific Northwest; The New Empire: Oregon, Washington, Idaho; Spokane Falls, Wash. Ty.: The Metropolis of Eastern Washington and Northern Idaho, 1889;* and *North-Western Industrial Exposition, Spokane Falls Official Catalogue* of 1890.

Gem Mine and Mill, Cañon Creek, Gem, Idaho, from the promotional brochure *Coeur d'Alene Towns*
Eastern Washington State Historical Society, Spokane, Washington

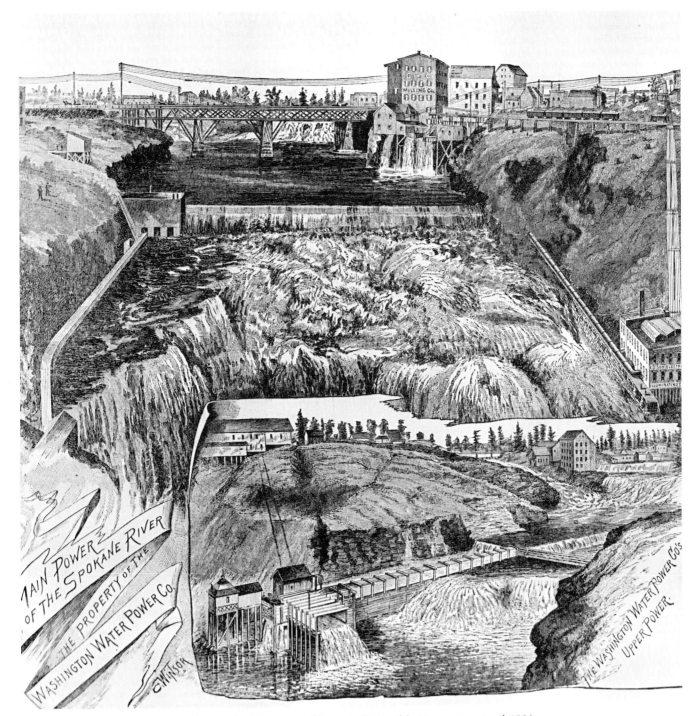

Spokane, Washington, in 1890 from *The Northwest Illustrated Monthly Magazine,* April 1890
Eastern Washington State Historical Society, Spokane, Washington

Waterpower was a recurring symbol of economic progress throughout the nineteenth century. Here is a somewhat fanciful drawing of the Washington Water Power Company's main plant on the Spokane River. Obviously, the illustration was designed to present a positive visual representation of Spokane as a center for industrial development.

99

Wallace, Idaho, from the promotional brochure *Coeur d'Alene Towns*
Eastern Washington State Historical Society, Spokane, Washington

As with most cities and towns on the western frontier, Wallace, Idaho, experienced a "Great Fire." This illustration shows the community before the conflagration of July 27, 1890.

On the "switchback" in the Cascade Mountains, Washington, from the promotional brochure Valley, Plain, and Peak— From Midland Lakes to Western Ocean, *1894*
Eastern Washington State Historical Society, Spokane, Washington

The Truth about the Palouse Country
Washington State University Libraries, Pullman, Washington

The Land that Lures: Summer in the Pacific Northwest
Washington State University Libraries, Pullman, Washington

The New Empire: Oregon, Washington, Idaho, a promotional brochure of the Oregon Immigration Board
Washington State University Libraries, Pullman, Washington

Spokane Falls, Wash. Ty., The Metropolis of Eastern Washington and Northern Idaho, 1889
Eastern Washington State Historical Society, Spokane, Washington

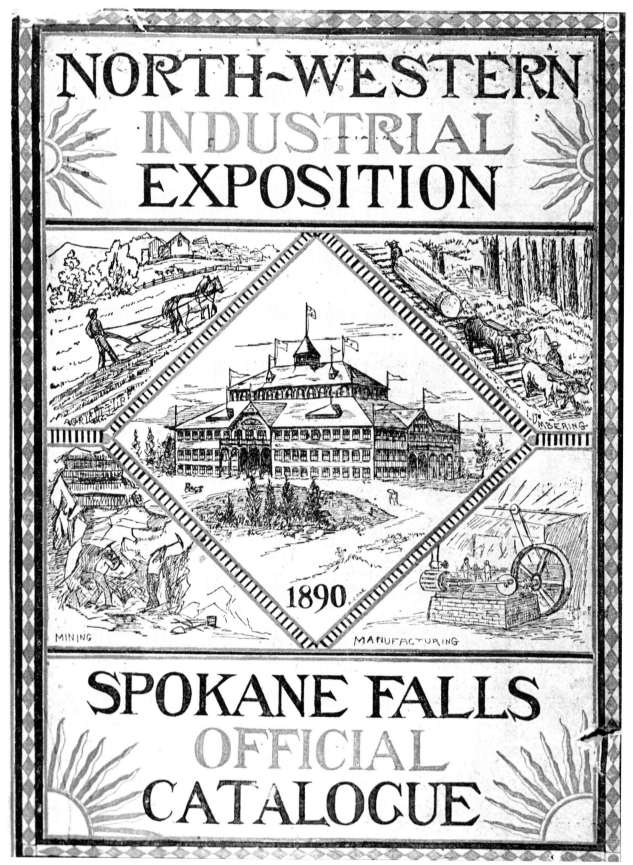

North-Western Industrial Exposition, 1890, Spokane Falls, Official Catalogue
Eastern Washington State Historical Society, Spokane, Washington

Wonderland Magazine, 1898
Eastern Washington State Historical Society, Spokane, Washington

Wonderland Magazine, 1899
Eastern Washington State Historical Society, Spokane, Washington

ELIZA R. BARCHUS, 1857-1959

By the end of the nineteenth century Eliza Barchus had become well known throughout the Pacific Northwest for her beautiful landscape oils. She received recognition for her work at both the 1887 and 1890 world's fairs and one of her canvases also received a gold medal at the 1905 Lewis and Clark Exposition.

Mt. Hood at Sunset by Eliza Barchus
Oregon Historical Society, Portland, Oregon

Hill's work spanned a period of more than fifty years. Best known as a landscape artist, she was accorded early acclaim for the oil paintings she completed for the Great Northern and Northern Pacific railroads. Hill was an outdoors' enthusiast roaming some of the most inaccessible regions of the Cascades in search of suitable scenes to capture on canvas.

Steilacoom, 1895 by Abby Williams Hill
University of Puget Sound Art Department, Tacoma, Washington

Peak near Lake Chelan called Mt. Booker

At the insistence of Mrs. Frank R. Hill, a Tacoma landscape painter, the United States Geological Survey has named a mountain peak near Lake Chelan Mt. Booker, named to honor Booker T. Washington, the famous Negro educator. The Geological Survey asserts that so far as it is concerned the selection of the name had no reference whatever to Booker T. Washington. The opposite idea prevails at the Tuskegee Institute.

Mrs. Hill asserted her belief that the name is essentially appropriate and expressed her confidence that race prejudice would take no umbrage against naming the Mt. after "the greatest colored man of the generation." She had traveled to Tuskegee Institute and had met with Mr. Washington.

The Mt. typified the uplifting work of Mr. Washington, founder and principal of Tuskegee Institute.

She painted the picture in 1904 and the U.S. Geological Survey gave her the honor of naming it, as it had never been named.

"What could be more fitting than to name it for one of the most truly great men of our times; great in soul, in serving the Lord through service to humanity, to whom no privation was too hard to bear no storm raging about him checked his purpose. He did not seek honor or commendation or fame, but they all came to him.

"When we look at Mt. Booker let us be thankful for Booker T. Washington's life. . . . His influence like the streams from the mountain will go through the ages to bless and help mankind."

Excerpt from the *Seattle Post-Intelligencer*, April 22, 1904

Mt. Booker near Lake Chelan, 1903 by Abby Williams Hill
University of Puget Sound Art Department, Tacoma, Washington

Columbia River, 1902 by Abby Williams Hill
University of Puget Sound Art Department, Tacoma, Washington

Mt. Rainier from Vashon Island, 1900 by Abby Williams Hill
University of Puget Sound Art Department, Tacoma, Washington

Willamette Falls by Joseph Drayton
Oregon Historical Society, Portland, Oregon

Peluse Falls by John Mix Stanley
Pacific Railroad Reports, volume 12, 1855-61

Scene on the Columbia, Oregon by John Mix Stanley
Amon Carter Museum of Western Art, Fort Worth, Texas

Sketchbook cover by James Madison Alden
Washington State Historical Society, Tacoma, Washington

Alden's sketchbook in the holdings of the Washington State Historical Society contains numerous drawings and water-colors of the Pacific Northwest.

Great Falls of the Palouse by James Madison Alden
National Archives, Washington D. C.

On returning from the 1860 boundary survey of the 49th parallel, Alden crossed the dry plateau country of the western Palouse. His watercolor of Palouse Falls is a product of the journey. The falls also were a favorite subject of other itinerant nineteenth-century artists, including Henry James Warre, Paul Kane, John Mix Stanley, and Gustavus Sohon.

View of Medical Lake from our Camp by Alfred Downing
Washington State Historical Society, Tacoma, Washington

Tongue Point, Early Morning by Cleveland Rockwell
Columbia River Maritime Museum, Astoria, Oregon

Mt. St. Helens from the Columbia River, 1879 by Cleveland Rockwell
Oregon Historical Society, Portland, Oregon

Selected Bibliography

Abbott, Carl. *The Great Extravaganza: Portland and the Lewis and Clark Exposition.* Portland: Oregon Historical Society, 1981.

Biddle, Nicholas, editor. *History of the Expedition under the Command of Captains Lewis and Clark, to the Sources of the Missouri, Thence across the Rocky Mountains and down the River Columbia to the Pacific Ocean . . . Prepared for the Press by Paul Allen, Esquire.* 2 volumes. Philadelphia: Bradford & Inskeep, 1814.

Bingham, Edwin R., and Glen A. Love, editors. *Northwest Perspectives: Essays on the Culture of the Pacific Northwest.* Seattle: University of Washington Press, 1979.

Catlin, George. *Episodes from "Life Among the Indians" and "Last Rambles."* Marvin C. Ross, ed. Reprint edition. Norman: University of Oklahoma Press, 1979.

_____. *Letters and Notes on the Manners, Customs, and Conditions of the North American Indians.* 2 volumes. New York: Dover, 1973.

_____. Mss. correspondence, Gilcrease Institute of American History and Art, Tulsa, Oklahoma.

Clark, Norman H. *Washington: A Bicentennial History.* New York: Norton, 1976.

Cox, Ross. *Adventures on the Columbia River.* London: Colburn, 1831.

Dodds, Gordon. *Oregon: A History.* New York: Norton, 1977.

Edwards, G. Thomas, and Carlos A. Schwantes, editors. *Experiences in the Promised Land: Essays in Pacific Northwest History.* Seattle: University of Washington Press, 1987.

Gass, Patrick. *A Journal of the Voyages and Travels of a Corps of Discovery, under the command of Capt. Lewis and Capt. Clarke . . . from the Mouth of the River Missouri through the Interior Parts of North America to the Pacific Ocean, during the years 1804, 1805, & 1806.* Pittsburgh: M'Keehan, 1807.

Goetzmann, William H. *Army Exploration and the American West, 1803-1863.* New Haven: Yale University Press, 1959.

_____. *Exploration and Empire: The Explorer and the Scientist in the Winning of the American West.* New York: Alfred A. Knopf, 1966.

_____. *New Lands, New Men, America and the Second Great Age of Discovery.* New York: Viking Press, 1986.

Goetzmann, William H., and William N. Goetzmann. *The West of the Imagination.* New York: W. W. Norton, 1986.

Harper, J. Russell. *Paul Kane's Frontier.* Austin: University of Texas Press, 1971.

Irving, Washington. *The Adventures of Captain Bonneville.* London: R. Bentley, 1837.

_____. *Astoria, or Anecdotes of an Enterprise beyond the Rocky Mountains.* London: Bentley, 1836.

Kane, Paul. *Wanderings of an Artist.* London: Longman's, 1859.

Lancaster, Samuel Christopher. *The Columbia: America's Great Highway.* Portland: Samuel Christopher Lancaster, 1915.

Lavender, David. *Land of Giants.* Garden City: Doubleday, 1956.

McGregor, Alexander Campbell. *Counting Sheep: From Open Range to Agribusiness on the Columbia Plateau.* Seattle: University of Washington Press, 1982.

Major-Frégau, Madeleine. *Overland to Oregon in 1845: Impressions of a Journey Across Canada.* Ottawa: Public Archives of Canada, 1976.

Meinig, Donald. *The Great Columbia Plain: A Historical Geography, 1805-1910.* Seattle: University of Washington Press, 1968.

Nicandri, David. *Northwest Chiefs: Gustav Sohon's Views of the 1855 Stevens Treaty Councils.* Tacoma: Washington State Historical Society, 1986.

Peterson, F. Ross. *Idaho: A History.* New York: Norton, 1976.

Powell, Fred Wilbur. *Hall Jackson Kelley, Prophet of Oregon.* Portland: Ivy Press, 1917.

Reps, John W. *Panoramas of Promise: Pacific Northwest Cities and Towns on Nineteenth-Century Lithographs.* Pullman: Washington State University Press, 1982.

Schimmel, Julia Ann. "John Mix Stanley and Imagery of the West in Nineteenth-Century Art," Ph.D. diss., New York University, 1983.

Stenzel, Franz. *Cleveland Rockwell, Scientist and Artist, 1837-1907.* Portland: Oregon Historical Society, 1972.

_____. *James Madison Alden: Yankee Artist of the Pacific Coast.* Fort Worth: Amon Carter Museum, 1975.

Stevens, Isaac I. *Reports of Explorations and Surveys to Ascertain the Most Practicable and Economical Route for a Railroad from the Mississippi River to the Pacific Ocean, 1853-1854.* 36th Cong., 1st sess., S. Ex. Doc. 78, Washington, D. C., 1860.

Viola, Herman J., and Carolyn Margolis, editors. *Magnificent Voyagers: The U.S. Exploring Expedition, 1838-1842.* Washington, D. C.: Smithsonian Institution, 1985.

Wagner, Henry R., and Charles Camp. *The Plains and the Rockies, 1800-1865.* 4th edition, revised, enlarged, and edited by Robert H. Becker. San Francisco: John Howell Books, 1984.

Wheat, Carl I. *Mapping the Transmississippi West.* 6 volumes. San Francisco: Institute of Historical Cartography, 1957-1963.